# Punk Rock Manifesto

*Look, Work, Accept, Transcend*

By Kimberlee Jensen Stedl

DISCLAIMER: This book is for self-knowledge and is not intended to prescribe any course of physical or psychiatric treatment. Please consult your physician before beginning a new physical conditioning program, especially if you have a pre-existing condition for which you are being treated or you have been inactive for a long period of time.

Published by 8th Element Yoga, a division of
8th Element Recreation LLC
2070 Cooper St.
Suite 122
Missoula, MT 59808

Published in Missoula, Montana, United States of America.

First edition: July 2010

ISBN-13: 978-0-615-37000-2
ISBN-10: 0-615-37000-4
Library of Congress Control Number: 2010933349
Library of Congress Classification: RA781.7.S743 2010
Dewey Decimal Classification: 613.7'046

**Visit us on the web at**

**PunkRockYoga.com**
**and**
**8thElementYoga.com**

*To my son Ivan, who has challenged me to practice
what I preach more than anything else ever has.*

# Contents

# Acknowledgements

I would like to thank the Vera Project in Seattle, and specifically Shannon Stewart, for all their support and for giving Punk Rock Yoga its first home. Thanks also to all the musicians and DJs who have come to play, and to all of the students who gave a new teacher a chance to try something new and unusual—I have learned a great deal from all of you. I also thank all the yoga teachers whose classes and trainings have enriched me personally and professionally.

I offer a huge thanks to all the Punk Rock Yoga teachers who have not only been excellent ambassadors for the missions and goals of Punk Rock Yoga, but have also deepened and expanded the philosophy with their unique perspectives. It may not take a village to write a book, but I wanted my village to help birth this book. I thank all my teachers for their contributions to this work, especially Erin Ball, Jeni O'Keefe, and Apryl Pipe for providing feedback and edits that gave me greater insight, and Brian Williams for writing a foreword that gave me tears.

I also am grateful for my husband Todd who has continued to believe in me, especially when I have my doubts, and who has pushed me to say what I truly believe, rather than what I think the yoga police wants to hear. Also, I sincerely appreciate all of the editorial scrutiny he applied to this book.

Special thanks go out to my mother Barbara, who came out to Missoula to entertain my two-year-old son while my husband and I completed the editing of this book.

Finally, I am blessed by my son Ivan, who has transformed my life more completely than anything else ever could.

# Foreword

I'll never forget the day I first heard about Punk Rock Yoga. I was sitting in my yoga teacher training, wondering if I was in over my head. Sadie, my teacher, was talking about ways to individualize teaching—to express our own ideas within the framework of traditional yogic thought. She mentioned Punk Rock Yoga, which was getting some attention in the press. A couple of people in the room made that face that I've seen many times since: a look of, "What the hell?" I might have made that face, too. Sadie asked us if we thought being yogis meant that we had to listen to Enya all the time. I didn't know for sure, but I knew that if I could never listen to my beloved Dresden Dolls or sing along to The Cramps again, I might have to reconsider my decision to become a yoga teacher. I went home that night and started thinking about all the things that inspired me. What would my message be when I started teaching? What would a class with me be like for my students?

I knew it would have music, and I knew that it would be music I wanted to hear. The truth is, I enjoy a strong, athletic yoga class, and the idea of moving through a 75-minute class with slow, "soothing," tinkly, new age music in the background filled me with irritation. The thought of indie rock, or jazz, or New Orleans funk playing while I led a class through a sequence of sweat-inducing poses, though, that made me excited to teach. I went to the Punk Rock Yoga website to see what it was all about.

That night I learned that Punk Rock Yoga wasn't just yoga to punk rock music. I had my mind blown by the clarity and scope of Kimberlee's vision. She was teaching yoga the way it was supposed to be taught, and that made me see that "punk" had a lot more to do with yoga than I had realized at first. I thought about how basic punk rock is, and that reminded me of how basic yoga should be. It doesn't need a whole lot of accoutrements, as the French might say. It just requires a willing student, and a knowledgeable teacher. I also decided that it sounded exactly like something I wanted to be involved in.

Punk Rock Yoga struck a chord in me before I even became a yoga teacher. I was taken by the ideals espoused by Kimberlee, Punk Rock Yoga's founder. I thought about the elitism in certain yoga studios here in New York City, and how people were paying more attention to their fancy yoga mat bags than they were to the way they spoke to a fellow student who might have accidentally stepped on their yoga mat. I thought about how in one particular yoga studio, the owner would frown at some of my male friends who came in wearing nail polish or had piercings. I remembered a teacher friend saying someone walked out of her class because she played 80's music one day, instead of the usual sitar.

I thought about how the behavior I was seeing actually ran counter to the most basic tenets of yoga. The Punk Rock Yoga website said "All types of music + all types of people + all types of yoga = Punk Rock Yoga." That equation was math even I could understand! I knew New York City needed a dose of yoga that came without judgment and celebrated all types of people. I also knew that I wanted to teach yoga that was powerful, fun, and respectful of tradition, while exploring new ways to interpret classical teachings. I wrote Kimberlee shortly after I completed my teacher training, and asked her if I could start a Punk Rock Yoga class in New York. It was one of the best decisions I have ever made.

I've been teaching the class for several years, and Punk Rock Yoga is really starting to catch on. We have moved from a grungy black box theater that had to be swept three times before each class to a beautiful space near Times Square. There's a church across the street that rings bells around the time we have our *savasana*. Yoga writers have reviewed the class. It was featured in a documentary for Japanese television, and I've even taught it as a free class in a certain well-known, corporate yoga apparel store. (I did say during that class that you could do yoga in a ratty pair of cut-offs just fine. I couldn't help it; it just sort of popped out!) I've tried to teach classes that are simple, challenging, and stay true to the real meaning of yoga, with no added "psychobabble."

During my class I try to remind people of their own greatness—a message I have always taken away from my conversations with Kimberlee. Kimberlee has become someone I look to for advice, and someone I consider a friend. She has a clear point of view, and a deep understanding of what yoga is really about. She gets it, and she explains it all here with no added bullshit.

This book will tell you what Punk Rock Yoga is all about. It's clear and easily understandable. If you read this book, you will know what you need to do to get on the yoga train, and ride it to your desired destination, whether you want to get physically stronger, or become "one with everything." (What did the yogi say at the hot dog stand? Make me one with everything.) You'll come away knowing the real meaning of yoga, and you'll be able to discuss it with anyone who asks. It's broken down and discussed in a clear-headed, logical manner. The book should be required reading for yoga teachers, in my opinion. This book is simple, profound, and a lot of fun to read.

There is a real hunger for this kind of sincere, simple yoga, and there's a tribe of students interested in looking beyond what many yoga studios are selling them. We encourage a do- it-yourself approach to yoga, and this book will serve as your call to action, your toolbox, and your inspiration to start along the beautiful, frustrating, inspiring, and completely rewarding path of yoga.

*Namaste,*

Brian Williams
Punk Rock Yoga and Core Strength Vinyasa Instructor
New York City

# About this book

You picked up this book for one of several reasons. 1) You consider yourself a punk of sorts and want to research ways to incorporate yoga into your life. 2) You have taken Punk Rock Yoga classes and want to delve deeper into the philosophy behind it. 3) Other yoga books did not resonate with you and you hope this book will. Or, perhaps, 4) you saw the title and thought, "Punk Rock Yoga? That's so crazy I just have to learn more!"

With this book, I aim to satisfy all those needs. We will explore yoga philosophy and discuss putting it to work in your day-to-day life—not the life of a yogi secluded in an ashram but rather your life, which involves work, bills, commuting, cleaning, and relatives. However, you will not find absolutes and platitudes; this is not a super simple self-help book. I sometimes say that I wish I could write one of those "the secret to success" or "seven easy steps to a happy life" books and laugh myself all the way to the bank. But I do not think in superficial platitudes and I bet you do not either. Instead, in this book you will find different perspectives to help you decide for yourself how to not only interpret yoga philosophy, but also how to utilize it. The yogic path is not a shortcut, but rather a framework for spiritual and psychological growth. However, if you crave a four-step plan, here is mine: "Look at your stuff, work on your stuff, accept your stuff, and transcend your stuff."

This book has been itching me for years. In October 2004, more than 50 newspapers in the United States ran an Associated Press article about Punk Rock Yoga, whereby they proclaimed it as "the latest fitness trend sweeping the nation" despite that at the time Punk Rock Yoga consisted of one weekly class in Seattle. Shortly afterward, I was approached by literary agents and drafted book proposals. After going through a couple of agents who met with little success and some publishers who would only publish me if I suddenly became best friends with rock stars, I decided to publish this book myself. By then, I had co-written and self-published two other yoga books (*Yoga for Scuba Divers* and *Yoga with a Friend*), so I was quite comfortable with the Do It Yourself publishing route.

When I finally got a head of steam to write this book I became pregnant with my first child, which put a rather large brake on my steamroller. In so many ways, having a child has truly tested my beliefs in what I say in class and in these pages. On some days, I seem to forget everything I have learned, yet on other days it is the only thing upon which I rely. As my son toddles around closer to independence, I notice he practices strong, audible breathing when stressed, having observed me for the past two years breathing my way through struggles. As I reviewed the pieces of this work I wrote for the proposals years ago, I still find my beliefs in these words, but now I have even more to contribute.

Deciding whether or not to include poses also proved a challenge. Though yoga is primarily a mental or psychological discipline, yoga also can involve a physical practice, which is what many people think is the sum total of yoga. The poses definitely help you slow down and focus, which boosts your mental discipline. They also have intrinsic physical benefits such as strength, balance, and flexibility. Practicing poses is wonderful for the body, and can help with your overall serenity, but if you stop there, I consider it yoga with a lowercase "y." To derive the full benefit from Yoga, I believe you need to strive to be a better person, living according to some practical behavioral guidelines, which we will discuss throughout this book.

When I stopped to really think about the book I wanted to write, the words of one of my guest Punk Rock Yoga teachers in Seattle kept echoing in my mind: "There are a million books out there on yoga poses, but it's your ideas about yoga that need to be heard." It's true—there are numerous books and videos illustrating poses and, to be blunt, a hamstring is a hamstring. However, books that break down the philosophy and relate it to the lives of urban Westerners are more scarce. Someday I do wish to release a pose book or DVD, but what needs to be written first is the manifesto.

I consider this book a manifesto in that I consider this book a call to action. My blustering stops at pretending this work will impact society in the manner of Karl Marx, but I hope it stirs something in you. At some points you may disagree and think me insane, but my hope is that those points prompt self-reflection. While yogic philosophy can be very esoteric, it can also be very practical and straightforward. I hope you find this book a useful application of that philosophy. I summarized some information because, in the nature of a manifesto, I wanted this to be a quick read, with actionable items you can put to use right away.

Focusing on philosophy also emphasizes what I consider the heart of yoga. Yoga is not something that you *do* once a week at a studio, but rather a way of who you can *be* when dealing with the world.

# A little Punk Rock Yoga history

When I started Punk Rock Yoga in 2003, I had a very simple goal: I hoped to create an atmosphere that would attract teenagers and other people who are not normally drawn to yoga. The class attracted crowds of all ages and what started as a small community service project has evolved into a nascent movement with numerous yoga teachers joining the fold. The more I taught and the more I immersed myself in the professional yoga community, the more I carved out a mission for Punk Rock Yoga: I want to scrub the elitism and rigidity out of modern yoga.

Punk Rock Yoga challenges stereotypes. It confronts the notion that punks are angry miscreants and that yogis are hippie contortionists. People are multifaceted and someone can be a punk and a yogi at the same time, yet many consider Punk Rock Yoga paradoxical. In fact, reactions to the name Punk Rock Yoga illustrate the absurdity of labels—by labeling someone you are drawing a box around that person, pigeonholing who you think they are, and denying the reality that people can be complex creatures.

Over the years, I have clarified my perspective to really consider Punk Rock Yoga in a broader sense—the philosophy really is DIY or Do It Yourself yoga. Of course, the punk rock movement popularized the DIY credo that motivated people to start their own record labels, magazines, clothing lines, and even form their own communities. The lesson of DIY is a lesson in self-reliance; the lesson of yoga is a lesson in self-teaching. Both the DIY credo and the teachings of yoga show people how to make their own way and take responsibility for their own lives.

So, does practicing yoga make you less of a punk? Does listening to punk rock make you less of a yogi or yogini? So-called purists in both camps will answer yes. They miss the point. You can be a punk, and a yogi, and anything else, but by defining yourself by a label you are denying your true self. Let go of your attachment to labels and boldly interpret for yourself.

# Get real

"What's this all about anyway?" Just about every religious and philosophical school tries to answer the meaning-of-life question. Yogic philosophy presents us with a theory on the nature of reality, which serves as a foundation for the behavioral guidelines and other aspects of yoga. This question, of course, is one that many of us wrestle with at some point in our lives, and the theories from yoga may provide you with additional insight, or at least additional questions to ask yourself.

The traditional yogic school of thought on reality is described in the foundational book of yoga philosophy, the *Yoga Sutras of Patanjali*. According to this philosophy, we can divide reality into two regions: everything we process with our five senses, considered nature (*prakriti*); and a higher consciousness (*purusha*). This higher consciousness is considered the divinity within all of us.

Yogis often talk about the concepts of *prakriti* and *purusha* in terms of the seen and the seer, respectively. A basic example is that as you watch ants crawling, they are the seen and you are the seer, often unbeknownst to the seen. In terms of our consciousness, sometimes you can actually observe yourself reacting in a negative way to something, witnessing your mind spin out of control. It is precisely this higher consciousness that allows you to step back and objectively observe the situation.

This view of reality teaches us that we have the capacity to transcend the day-to-day. We have a spirit that goes beyond paying bills, being stuck in traffic, having political arguments, and getting paper cuts. We all have a higher consciousness—what is considered to be our true self—but mental fluctuations (*citta*) get in the way of clarity. When you find your mind as turbulent as an ocean during a hurricane, just stop everything. Stop and breathe. Instead of reacting with a rush of adrenaline, taking a moment to breathe helps you collect yourself and tap into a higher, more rational mindset. If you are not facing an emergency, but find yourself swirling in an emotional storm, stop and breathe for a long period of time: practice yoga poses, go for a walk, sit and meditate, go for a bike ride—do something to clear your mind and tap into your higher state.

Yogic philosophy also considers our natural world an illusion (*maya*). In other words, our body is just an impermanent mass, but we all possess a higher, eternal self. If you have attended a yoga class, or visited India, you probably have heard the greeting *namaste*, which has several translations, including, "The divinity within me honors the divinity within you." Please note that the yogic view of divinity does not involve the worship of a particular god, but instead is a somewhat less tangible concept of divinity, more along the lines of an eternal, universal spirit. My favorite translation of *namaste* is, "Everything that is light and good within me recognizes everything that is light and good within you, and that is the place where our souls meet."

This concept of souls meeting is important to the concept of our higher self. In the yogic viewpoint, all of us share the same higher self, and we share it with the entire universe. You may not believe that, and that is okay, but the critical lesson is to recognize that everyone has this same capacity, regardless of skin color, gender, etc. You can view *maya* as the grand illusion of the superficial qualities that divide us, and *purusha*, or the transcendent self, as the commonality that unites us.

I believe that you do not have to fully accept the yogic definition of the nature of reality to practice yoga. Even if you doubt the concept of *purusha*, the ten behavioral guidelines of the restraints (*yamas*) and actions (*niyamas*) described in the *Yoga Sutras of Patanjali* can teach us how to live a better life. In fact, given that yoga is a tradition of contemplation, my hope is that after serious study you will reach your own conclusions to the question, "What is this all about anyway?"

# Discover the eight limbs

In the *yoga sutras*, Patanjali laid out an eight-fold program for liberation called royal (*raja*) yoga. Here are the limbs of royal yoga in the order presented by Patanjali:

- restraints (*yamas*),

- actions (*niyamas*),

- practice of physical postures (*asana*),

- control of our vital energy through breath (*pranayama*),

- withdrawal from the five senses (*pratyahara*),

- concentration and focus (*dharana*),

- meditation (*dhyana*),

- liberation (*samadhi*).

Take note that the first two limbs address our day-to-day actions, rather than just the time we take for our pose practice. The restraints and actions are lifestyle guidelines that are the most accessible limbs and easiest to discuss, yet they can also be the most challenging.

People have interpreted the restraints and actions in some radically different ways. The controversies arise because the *Yoga Sutras of Patanjali* provides sparse explanation of its tenets. This leeway has spawned vigorous debate in the yoga community as to the real meanings of each restraint and action. Patanjali wrote the *sutras* as abridged notes, in part because yogis were expected to discuss these principles with their gurus, and so that people could interpret the concepts for themselves. This room for debate separates yoga from more strictly defined philosophical paths, which makes it even more intriguing to me—internal and external debate leads to growth.

That yoga poses comprise only one-eighth of the total yoga picture often surprises devoted yoga-class goers. Some purists say you are not practicing yoga if all you ever do is attend a yoga pose class. While that might be technically true, so what? If just attending a yoga class helps you with your mental health and it makes you a better person, that may be all you need out of yoga. Because you are reading this book, though, I assume you want more, and yoga can offer much more, meeting you where you are when you are ready. You can someday move to India and live a monastic life in an ashram, or you can take this wisdom and apply it to your own life to help you find clarity, peace, happiness, and liberation. I call this Yoga with a capital "Y."

When learning yoga philosophy, the middle path of moderation underlies all of these guidelines. For example, when following the guideline of purity, you should keep yourself clean, but not develop obsessive-compulsive disorder and wash your hands every five minutes. Even non-violence has a moderate tone: you should avoid harming all living things as much as possible, but not to the point where pacifism means letting other people abuse you. We can imagine the restraints and actions as a continuum, and that spot in the middle is where you want to be.

# Control yourself: yoga restraints (*yamas*)

As we jump onto the first limb of Patanjali's royal yoga, behavioral restraints (*yamas*), we immerse ourselves in perhaps the most challenging aspect of yoga—how to be a better person. The five restraints are non-violence (*ahimsa*), non-lying (*satya*), non-stealing (*asteya*), non-excess (*brahmacharya*), and non-possessiveness (*aparigraha*).

Yogis did not invent restraints: many cultural groups believe in controlling our behavior. Several religions practice regular fasting to purify the body for holy days. Mormons obey behavior codes that include abstinence from numerous chemicals, including caffeine. The Straight Edge movement—born in the early 1980's out of the punk movement—advocated the Minor Threat creed, "don't drink/don't smoke/don't fuck." Since then, the movement has moved in several directions including vegan diets and environmental activism that parallel some of the movements in yoga.

Yogis practiced abstinence thousands of years before most of these groups emerged. Yogis practice these restraints to clear their minds so they can experience liberation (*samadhi*). However, the principle of moderation guides everything in yoga, and many yogis make a distinction between restraint and absolution. You can restrain yourself without abstaining. This is a critical point to understanding the restraints. As you read through these, keep in mind that these guidelines are intended to make your life better, not to make you miserable.

Yogis do not believe in guilt—just practice and evolution. Here's a fun bit of trivia: no scholar has discovered a Sanskrit word that translates to guilt. Many yoga teachers have deduced that guilt never entered the vocabulary because it is a pointless concept. So as you read these restraints, examine your behavior with this one thought in mind: what you did in the past is over. We can only look forward and resolve to do things differently in the future. Who you are and who you can be evolves with every passing moment. Examine the past as a guide, or a reference point, and resolve to change the things you think need changing in the present. Remember, only you can really know what you should change.

# Non-violence (*ahimsa*)

Definition: "In the presence of one firmly established in non-violence, all hostilities cease."—*Yoga Sutras of Patanjali*, translation and commentary by Sri Swami Satchidananda

This one sentence summarizes the principle to which Gandhi dedicated his life. Non-violence is the root of all the restraints and actions: once you firmly plant your feet in a non-violent or compassionate life, the rest will follow. Practicing non-violence involves much more than refraining from outward acts of aggression—it means refraining from violent thoughts and finally, replacing hostility with love. On paper, this looks simple, but in practice this means stopping yourself from thinking "jerk" (or something stronger) when someone irritates you in traffic. I struggle with this myself, particularly when dealing with grief. My pattern was to avoid sorrow and replace it with anger. Slowly, but surely, I have learned to catch myself in the act.

So, how do you avoid those thoughts? One trick is to step back for a moment, take a breath, and evaluate the situation. You can consider the present situation that has you so enraged in the context of your whole life or the sum total of the earth's existence and evaluate the true impact. The world will continue to spin on its axis. The yogic theory of reality gives us perspective in that we have to look beyond our superficial self to recognize our true, impermeable self. The person who just cut you off in traffic does not define who you really are. The only person who can change who you are inside is you, not the random stranger in the motorized metal box. The more introspection and meditation you do, the more you learn to separate the transitory and superficial world from your long-term self.

Non-violence also applies to how we treat ourselves. If you can look beyond the mirror and see your inner self, your true self, you will find that it is not fat, ugly, pimply, or any of those labels. Look beyond the mirror, and you will see an inner light. This takes extra effort for younger people because they are bombarded with these awful messages. If you just remember these messages are merely mirages, you can stop internalizing and repeating hurtful yet meaningless words.

In addition, non-violence also means not being a victim of violence. It means getting as far away as you can from a physically or verbally abusive relationship. Nobody deserves that. We tend to have an overdeveloped fear of change, which can keep people in victim mode. Contrary to the popular saying, I believe the devil you know is worse than the devil you don't know. Everyone deserves a life free from violence, no matter how difficult change can be.

Beyond not being violent and not being victims of violence, we have a responsibility of saving others from violence. Many disagree with this interpretation. Some say, "I practice yoga, so I can't get involved." Yoga is not an excuse for cowardice or laziness. To me, non-violence means speaking out about genocide, petitioning for tougher rape laws, boycotting countries with abysmal human rights records, protesting unjust wars, lobbying against economic inequities, etc. I cannot tell you what to believe, but I can tell you that violence wins only when people do nothing. If you think that you are powerless, I encourage you to watch the documentary *Weapons of the Spirit* by Pierre Sauvage. A French community of 5,000 people in France managed to rescue 5,000 Jewish people from the Nazis between 1940 and 1944. The farmers shared their limited resources, often going without meals themselves, and risked their lives. This is my favorite tale of humble people doing heroic things. While they might not have studied yoga, they exemplified non-violence. They were true gurus of *ahimsa*.

People have interpreted non-violence in other ways. Some people believe non-violence includes non-violence against animals, and that you must adopt a vegan lifestyle. They believe that if we are complicit in the suffering of animals for our shoes, our meals, our vaccines, and our cosmetics, then we are not practicing the principle of non-violence and therefore not really doing yoga. Sharon Gannon and David Life, founders of the Jivamukti studio in New York, unequivocally declare this position in their book, *Jivamukti Yoga*. Many in the yoga community share that view, as gurus throughout time have advocated this lifestyle. This is, however, their interpretation—nowhere in the *yoga sutras* does any discussion of vegetarianism or veganism appear.

I follow a middle path on the animal rights question, believing that biologically some people need animal meat for food, but that testing cosmetics on animals, using animals for sport fighting, and other uses of animals that fail to provide sustenance is cruel and unnecessary. I also believe people should truly examine the act of eating meat and not just eat meat because that's what their parents fed them.

I respect the cycle-of-life concept and try to look at a bigger picture, including the sum total of impact. A local fisherman in

Thailand has probably done less to harm fish than me eating my frozen, processed, vegan tofu dish, considering all the environmental resources it took to prepare and delivery that food to me. Also, this question for me often brings up first-world narcissism: it's quite easy to live a vegan lifestyle when you live in a city filled with food alternatives and you have the money to make those choices, but to judge those in radically different environments for not doing the same shows a lack of compassion.

I had been a vegetarian for 16 years. In fact, it was my interpretation of the Bible that caused me to give up meat. I interpreted "Thou shalt not kill," to include animals. However, I eventually developed an intolerance to soy and found it difficult to get adequate protein from plant-based sources. More importantly, I wanted to bear a child and after lots of research I realized that pregnancy and breastfeeding required much more protein than my current vegetarian diet provided. So I finally added fish to my diet. I struggled with this decision for a full year. I further decided to expose my son to meat and in fact noticed a dramatic improvement in his sleep when I started feeding him meat rich with heme iron. I will not generalize that an omnivore diet is the only way for children, but I do believe a child's dietary needs to be very different from those of a fully-grown woman.

Have I conveniently changed my ethics? Perhaps, but even when I practiced strict vegetarianism I always believed it was the right choice for me at the time, and that just as I had every right to eat according to my beliefs, so too did others. Our diet is ultimately our choice, but the practice of yoga insists that we contemplate it, examine it, and enact it with minimal suffering. There are choices for omnivores, such as animals raised in the most sustainable and humane methods possible. The critical component is that we fully understand our choices and minimize our impact on the life around us.

We begin by taking responsibility for our choices. Yes, the world is a mighty big place and no, choosing meatless hot dogs will not bring back lost herds of buffalo, but lots of little things by lots of people add up to big things. You can follow a path of moderation by buying cage-free eggs, free-range meat, and wild-caught fish; you can and should also expand your horizons to include beans and other plant-based protein sources. According to the Association for the Advancement of Science, the amount of meat consumed by the average United States citizen is more than three times the global average—there's plenty of fat to be trimmed. But reducing the amount of food we waste is even more critical. While the Indian traditions say never to eat leftovers and only to eat freshly cooked food, I find it morally compelling to organize enough to avoid throwing out food daily. Native Americans would use almost every part of an animal, showing reverence for the act of taking a life. That ethos needs to enter our consciousness when choosing our food.

In addition, we can minimize the suffering of animals by prosecuting people for animal cruelty and outlawing the testing of cosmetics and other non-essentials on animals. I have mixed feelings on testing medical treatments on animals. Liver disease research done on rats helped me fight a life-threatening illness, which is only one example of how medical research on animals has benefited me. From a pragmatic standpoint, I believe we should develop technology to eliminate the need for animal testing. Until then, I believe we need to scrutinize research and balance objectives for the greater good.

This might sound like relative ethics to some purists, but in fact everyone practices situational ethics. While we may consider ourselves as pacifists, we cannot be certain that we would not take the life of an animal, or another human for that matter, when faced with a life-threatening situation. Also, we need to ask just how far do we take the concept of non-violence regarding animal welfare. For example, do we forego swatting a biting mosquito to protect its life? What if a mother did so but ultimately died from malaria that was passed to her from the mosquito, leaving her children to suffer? Swatting the mosquito does not mean she failed to practice non-violence, it means she examined her conscience and put her duty (*dharma*) as a mother first. I use an extreme example to illustrate that we all make decisions regarding the lives of flora and fauna daily and that we must balance the greater impact of our actions. Even the yogic practice of using a neti pot kills bacteria and viruses, which are living creatures. This does not mean we can kill indiscriminately, but rather that we need to examine all our actions and determine the potential harm and balance that against true necessity.

Every human being impacts the earth. I have conversed with people so obsessed with a light footprint they virtually regret being born. Of course we should tread as lightly as we can, but think of how pointless it is to lament our own births. Extremism, even for what appears to be a righteous cause, is poison. Moderation is the antidote.

Drawing absolute lines is easier in many ways than pondering difficult ethical choices. It's easy to draw lines in the sand until you actually step into it and feel it between your toes. For example, in balancing the notions of "celebrating diversity" versus "saving the planet" we run into conflict. Do we celebrate high birth rates in groups such as Hispanic Americans as part of their culture, or do we criticize it as unsustainable development? That does present a conundrum.

A culture argument often arises concerning violence against women. People justify violent and unnecessary practices against women, such as "honor killings" by saying that we must respect the culture of other people. The teachings of yoga could certainly help heal these crises—if only people could let the past remain in the past, see that a woman has a pure spirit despite her body being violated, and realize that being overly concerned with your neighbors' opinions is a deceit, then perhaps these rape victims would not have to be slaughtered just so the family can save face. Even the birthplace of yoga, India, struggles with gender- and class-based violence.

In order to fully practice non-violence, I believe that everyone should work towards changing the cultural norms that tolerate violence against people. From a yoga standpoint, the nature of culture is impermanent and forever changing, so people should work to make their culture more peaceful and egalitarian for all. In the United States, for example, owning slaves was once part of the culture, but doing so now would be considered morally reprehensible, demonstrating that cultural change for the benefit of humanity is possible.

Now, one might question why I can tolerate the killing of an animal but not the killing of a human being. I see a huge distinction in the slaughter of a person because of hatred versus slaughtering a cow to feed people. I also draw a distinction between killing wolves for sport and killing an elk to feed a family. Similarly, I see a distinction between killing a woman so her family can erase the shame of her being a rape victim versus helping someone suffering from terminal cancer end their life. Rather than seeing an absolute that all killing is wrong, I draw the line that killing, without gratitude, frugality, and reverence, is wrong. I examine the root of non-violence and try to determine whether the killing was done out of necessity or done out of hostility. Of course, you should examine your own conscious about these issues and reach your own interpretations or conclusions.

Perhaps we have discussed too many unpleasant issues for a yoga book, but I truly believe that the hardest work in yoga is in defining our personal moral code. Though the work continues perpetually, we have a firm place to start. Once we begin treating ourselves with love and dignity, we can find it easier to treat everyone else in the same way. Letting go of anger is the first step towards liberation. However, I must reemphasize the important distinction that letting go of anger does not mean you stop taking action; instead, it means that you take action without letting the hostility consume you for days afterward.

In a self-defense class taught by a Seattle non-profit organization called Home Alive, I learned a very effective de-escalation and boundary-setting technique that applies here. The technique has four steps to dealing with a problem: 1) name the behavior, 2) repeat naming the behavior, 3) direct the behavior, and 4) end it. Imagine your upstairs neighbors blast their stereo and wake you up. Instead of stewing for a while, you can immediately phone or knock on their door and name the behavior by stating, "I can hear your stereo in my apartment and we are now in quiet hours." That alone may get someone to change as this step is all about alerting someone to an invasive behavior without attaching blame. If they do not, then you repeat what you just said, because they may not have heard or understood you the first time. If that still does not work, you move on to directing the behavior by saying something like, "Please turn your stereo down." If that still does not work you, end it by phoning the authorities. If this behavior continues nightly, then you may have to truly end it by getting your city government involved, buying a white noise machine, or even moving if necessary. The critical component to setting boundaries is to take action immediately without hostility. I find that the longer I let a problem go, the more time I have to attach emotions, so taking immediate action while staying calm, and without attaching any motive to the other person's behavior, is the best way I have found to successfully set boundaries.

Yes, of course, at some point in your development you might possibly be able to transcend all distractions and sleep in the loudest of environments, but initially it's unrealistic—even ancient yogis sequestered themselves in quiet spots for rest. Tibetan monks do not learn their renowned meditation skills by starting in a noisy city. If you are just beginning your yoga journey you start with baby steps, and the first step towards liberation is moving beyond hostility. To do so, I believe, you first learn how to address conflict and stand up for yourself and others without anger, hatred, or violence.

**Incorporating non-violence in your yoga poses:** First, you should be kind to your body by discerning between muscle fatigue and pain. You want to challenge your body without beating it up. Also, remember the principle of non-violence when you evaluate your poses. If you struggle, so what? Some poses take years of work, while others may only take days. Instead of bashing yourself with negative thoughts, replace them with positives. Think, "I am getting stronger and more flexible every day."

# Non-lying (*satya*)

*Satya* (SAH-tyah)

Definition: "To one established in truthfulness, actions and their results become subservient."—*Yoga Sutras of Patanjali*, translation and commentary by Sri Swami Satchidananda

*Satya*, or truthful speech and actions, first requires you to find the truth. In yoga, the truth is considered oneness with the eternal spirit. Once you connect your conscious with "the truth" then you will always speak the truth. Instead of viewing this concept through an anthropomorphized lens, I have come to view the yogic concept of this spirit as more of an idea. Personally, I try to see this universal soul as something very pure, as in when you experience a flash of pure, unselfish love for another person. You can also imagine it as a powerful, eternal, and universal force that knows not physical and temporal boundaries. Yoga does not ask that you subscribe to any particular religion or belief system. All that yoga asks is that you realize your true self, which is united with something that transcends your current situation. Your true self is boundless and eternal. Your true self is unaffected by transitory things like bills, zits, and traffic.

Once we begin to see that that the daily, worldly self does not limit who we really are, we begin to see this same eternal force in others around us. Several things jump out at me when I contemplate the truth in yoga. Racism is a lie. If I am really part of a universal truth, or universal spirit, then so is my neighbor. Since we are both one with this universal spirit, and since skin color is an impermanent condition, I cannot judge her based on the color of her skin because doing so is a lie—the truth is that we are all one. As I teach my son about eating fruit, I also teach him lessons of our true nature: we have to dig through the bitter skin to access the nourishing, juicy stuff inside. Bigotry of all sorts is a lie, because gay or straight, black or white, man or woman, elderly or young, we are the same inside. In the yogic perspective, wherever you are right now is where you need to be. So if you happen to be gay, right now you are meant to be gay. When you align with the truth of an eternal spirit you transcend all labels.

As a meditative exercise, go to a park, or another public space, and sit quietly with your eyes shut for several minutes, visualizing a pure light glowing inside of you. Try to see yourself as simply pure light. Then, open your eyes and try seeing the same light glowing in other people. This takes a lot of work, but give it a shot. If this visualization doesn't work for you, try to see that everyone has two lungs, just like you. Just for one day, try looking at everyone around you as being of the same essence inside. Once you find this truth, you can truly speak the truth. If you are truthful, and see others as sharing the same eternal force that you do, then non-violence will naturally follow.

"The only way to tell the truth is to speak with kindness. Only the words of a loving man can be heard."—Henry David Thoreau

We distinguish between real honesty and the "Can I be honest with you?" mean-spiritedness, which some people masquerade as honesty. Real honesty can only come when we are truthful with ourselves, not when we are using honesty as an excuse for cruelty. Too often we do not speak the truth. For example, when a teenager yells to his parents, "I wish you were dead," that is not the truth. The truth is that he is angry about something, like his parents not buying him a new video game console. (Notice that often our attachments—especially to material things—cause such pain.) Truthful speech does not mean blurting out things in anger; it means getting to the heart of the matter. This concept can improve your communication, as many bitter arguments mask the truth of frustration. Often we will argue about a superficial topic when really something deeper is the problem. Before feuding with someone in your life, reflect deeply on the source of your anger. Of course, once you can get to the source of the anger, you can work to transcend it, but the first step is awareness.

Realistically, getting to that level of liberation—where we remain as peaceful as a mountain lake at sunrise no matter what the situation—takes tremendous dedication and time. I often tell my classes to look at our evolution as over a lifetime, or perhaps multiple lifetimes. But before we can get there, we must face our emotional warts first, and it's much better to face your memories once they surface than to bury them even further. Yogis call these deep memories *samskara*, or mental impressions, and use the process of yoga to first face these mental impressions, then liberate themselves from the impressions. Trust that you can handle anything you unlock, trust that you can get help to cope with what you have long suppressed, and trust that as you liberate the emotions trapped inside, you will liberate yourself.

People spend thousands of dollars on psychiatrists while probing for the truth. "What's really bothering you?" The sources of our grief often lie encrusted in plates of safety buffers. The meditative practices of yoga often uncover deep-rooted thoughts and ideas. When you begin a process of deep meditation and exploration, I recommend reaching out when intense memories resurface. Most yoga teachers are not qualified in this realm. (Some yoga teachers do have degrees in psychiatric counseling, but most do not.) A good yoga teacher can definitely mentor you through the process, but if something comes up and knocks the crap out of you, I think you should find a professional to help you through it. You do not have to spend your lifetime in therapy, but you should take time to really dig in and figure out what lies beneath.

However, this runs contrary to everything written in the *Hatha Yoga Pradipika*, a foundational yoga book written in the 15th century. The *Hatha Yoga Pradipika* states that yogis should only practice under strict tutelage of a guru and that yogis should trust the guru completely. While I agree that a guru is an incredible gift, and that attending yoga classes definitely helps with the physical practice, I don't believe that most yoga teachers are qualified to counsel someone struggling with past physical abuse, for example. That is outside of the scope of practice for most teachers and is outside the training most instructors receive.

If you seek help from a close friend instead, just make sure your friend is honestly willing to help. Sometimes friends mean well but have ulterior motives. For example, you might feel distraught over something and decide to stay in on a Saturday, but your friend might rush over and cheer you up and convince you that partying will make you feel better. Your friend could be right, depending on the intensity of your emotions. Your friend probably does care, but at that moment she might care more about going out herself than she does about your emotions, and perhaps she does not want to go out alone. As long as she is attached to going out, she cannot truly put your interests first.

Sadly, we spend way too much time defining ourselves by falsehoods. We are not our cars, our jackets, or even our tattoos. Yoga teaches us to control the fluctuations of the mind (*citta*). These fluctuations lead us to project onto ourselves a false portrait of what we truly are. Ultimately, we are eternal light, eternal sound, and eternal energy. Ultimately, we are no different from what we consider sacred and divine. You can begin by letting go of your attachments and stop identifying yourself with the impermanent. Of course you have to work to pay your bills, but the minute you define yourself by your work, you are lying.

When I meet people at a party they will often ask, "What do you do?" which, given some of my employment history, I consider the least interesting aspect of who I am. I often answer, "I do many things," and then when I get asked the follow up question, "But what do you do for a living?" I will answer, "Do you want to know what I do that makes me feel alive, or what I do to pay the bills?" (I admit to losing a conversation partner on several occasions.) Many of us have jobs that do not fuel our spirit; they are not what we do to live, but without them we could not eat.

Some people advocate utopias where everyone is an artist, which sounds lovely in theory, but someone needs to haul the garbage and clean the sewers. If everyone spent their days just creating art, we would live amongst piles of garbage and rivers of wastewater. Of course you should pursue a job that you love—but even a dream job is not a sum total of who you are as a person.

Even people with truly honorable jobs, such as those working for Doctors Without Borders, need to practice some detachment from their jobs. Their jobs are transitory—there was a time when they were not doctors and there will be a time when they will no longer be doctors; who they really are cannot be contained in a mere title.

Next time you meet someone at a party, instead of asking them, "What do you do?" ask them, "Who are you?" or "What would you like me to know about you?" If they look at you strangely, so be it. Ask yourself, "Who am I?" and try to answer without using labels. When we define ourselves by our work, our romantic partners, our youth, or other temporary situations, then we feel tremendous loss when we lose those external things. But when we realize the truth, that we have something greater and more permanent inside ourselves than our work, then we lose our attachment to our labels and can face change without fear.

**Incorporating truth into your yoga poses:** Be honest with yourself in the poses. If a pose feels too easy, try to recruit more muscle activity, go deeper in the pose, or lengthen your breaths. If you feel the body tremble, recognize that you have gone too far and back off from the pose. Also, you can practice truthfulness by keeping your focus on the present moment; focusing on your breath will help you keep your focus. In some poses, you can close your eyes and fix your internal gaze on the space inside your head just behind the center of your brow. Yogis consider this the center of intuition and inner knowledge.

# Non-stealing (*asteya*)

*Asteya* (ah-STAY-yah)

Definition: "To one established in non-stealing, all wealth comes."—*Yoga Sutras of Patanjali*, translation and commentary by Sri Swami Satchidananda

In its simplest form, non-stealing means just that—don't hijack a car. Non-stealing and truth often work hand-in-hand because many people lie in order to steal. Cheating on your taxes is stealing from your fellow citizens. We could spend the entire book discussing whether or not the government deserves our money, but that is irrelevant. When people—including those who run big corporations—lie and cheat on their taxes, ultimately someone else ends up paying, either by a tax increase elsewhere or by a cut in benefits. Too often, the benefits that get cut are usually the ones that go to the people most in need.

Some people might condone stealing from "the man." Unlike Robin Hood, many who steal from the rich generally don't turn around and give to the poor. Instead of stealing, I say find an alternative. However, I must make a big distinction about a desperate mother who steals a few oranges to feed her kids and a wealthy person who steals because he can get away with it. Yogic philosophy teaches us to take responsibility. We all share in this world and we have a duty to treat others equitably.

Most people do not steal outright, but rather might cross some fine lines. For example, if a waiter forgets to add an item onto your bill—not explicitly giving you a complimentary item, but rather simply forgetting—it might be tempting to think that you got something for free. But, that item will cost the restaurant owner, or it may even cost the waiter his job if the owner treats her employees harshly. It might tempt you to think that you "scored," but this dishonesty is a form of stealing. It may mean very little monetarily to the restaurant owner, but to our soul, honesty means everything.

To understand why some of us give into temptations like this, we need to examine the root of stealing—an attachment to our stuff, which is impermanent. Stuff is just stuff; it does not liberate us. In fact, quite the opposite—stuff imprisons us because we get trapped in the acquisition and protection of stuff. We all need food, shelter, and clothing and I like having great music and books as well, but ultimately it's the actions we take to acquire stuff, and our relationships with our stuff—not the stuff itself—that shapes us.

I have read of people who have taken hardcore pledges to not buy anything besides necessities like food, light bulbs, and toilet paper for one full year. While they reported the exercise a challenge, they all reported a great sense of liberation. Such thrift may not be practical as a lifelong practice—nor is it a middle path—but we can learn a lesson of frugality in that the less time we spend acquiring non-essential items, the more time we have for more rewarding pursuits.

Even beyond actions, the concept of non-stealing also translates into avoiding jealousy and competitiveness. Instead of looking at your neighbor's house and thinking, "If I only had money like them, I could be happy too," think, "Let me find a way to be happy right here and now." Often our jealousy manifests as negativity and cynicism. We think, "Sure, she's really skinny and pretty, but I bet she's bulimic." Instead, and I admit this is hard, we should look at ourselves and think, "I'm not so bad myself." Or, on a deeper level think, "On the inside, we are all the same, so at the fundamental level there is no difference between us."

We should all work as hard as we can in all our endeavors, but we should avoid comparisons against others. We can compete without succumbing to competitiveness. For example, in my youth I participated in triathlons. I always thought to myself, "I hope I win," but then when it was apparent I would not win I thought, "Well, I hope I'm not last." My insecurity needed at least one person to finish after me to validate my performance. No one wants to be the low man on the totem pole. This is the foundation of racism—everyone feels the need to be higher than at least one other person or group of people. Extreme competitiveness leads to pain. We escape this trap by returning to the fundamental truth that we all share the same universal spirit, which outlasts any sort of competition.

I have struggled with this concept myself. When I began my yoga teacher training, I could not do some poses very well. As the instructor began showing us poses, I secretly wished others would struggle, so that I would not feel so bad about struggling myself. Of course, I resented myself for having those jealous thoughts, so I have worked very hard on this principle. The more I learned about the true point of the poses—preparing your body for meditation, creating a moving meditation, and discovering things about yourself—the more I was able to let go of my competitiveness. I continue to work on this concept, but I can report that now when I watch students in my class, or attend teacher trainings and other people's classes, I have learned to celebrate and be inspired by the success of others, even in poses that confound me.

**Incorporating non-stealing into your yoga poses:** Some day, pick up a copy of *Yoga Journal*, a well-known yoga magazine. As you examine some very tall and thin models in full extensions of advanced poses, see them as beautiful and inspiring. As you practice a version of the pose, see your version as equally beautiful and inspiring. Celebrate the fact that you are both doing the pose in the exact expression right for you. Yogic philosophy says that where you are right now is exactly where you need to be. If that differs from the models in *Yoga Journal*, so what? You are meant to walk in your own shoes, not someone else's. Everyone has their own body history filled with breaks, tears, and scars. Everyone is born with his or her own anatomical deviations from the norm in some way. You cannot change that, but you can make the best of what you have and move from jealousy towards admiration and inspiration.

# Non-excess (*brahmacharya*)

*Brahmacharya* (brah-mah-CHAHR-yah)

Definition: "By one established in continence, vigor is obtained."—*Yoga Sutras of Patanjali*, translation and commentary by Sri Swami Satchidananda

The yogis define *brahmacharya* as celibacy, or controlling your vital sexual energy. The Straight Edge people believed in abstaining from casual sex, because obsession with sex can really mess with your head. Like some in the Straight Edge movement, many yogis throughout history have advised abstaining from sex completely. However, more moderate interpretations of yoga philosophy—my interpretation included—consider the obsession with sex, not the act of sex itself, as the problem.

Ancient yogis knew that semen and vaginal secretions contain the origin of life. They believed that having sex constantly meant wasting this vital life energy—by wasting semen without fertilizing an egg, you were wasting a potential life. Many of the yogic texts were written for people pursuing a monastic life. The texts refer to married men (women were not part of the yoga world originally) as "householders," which implied people who have sex.

Many current yogis advise you to abstain from pre-marital sex and to limit the amount of sex once you are married. Christian leaders say the same thing. Of course, that restricts the idea of sex to just heterosexuals and homosexuals living in a limited number of U.S. states and countries where gay marriage is legal, which is why I personally disagree with the restriction of marriage. Intimacy between two people in love has an incredible healing power, but sex without any spiritual connection can be destructive.

The *yoga sutras* say that monastic life helps you concentrate because you have liberated your mind from the constant pursuit of sex. Let's face it, when you are taking an economics class, you cannot really digest the material if you spend the whole time fantasizing about the person sitting next to you. If you spend hours every day watching porn, you don't have much time for meditation or any other pursuits. So, instead of reading this as abstaining, think of it as eliminating the obsessive quality of sex.

The theme throughout all of these guidelines is moderation. If you moderate the amount of time you think about sex you will find so much brainpower free to focus on creative endeavors. Jon Waters demonstrated this concept in his film *Cecil B. Demented.* In the film, Cecil is a director making an independent film along with several of his devotees. He instructed the entire crew to abstain from sex until they finished, asking them to channel their sexual energy into making the film. Regardless of the film's unusual characters or chaotic ending, Jon Waters understood the principle of continence.

If you struggle with this issue, try this for an experiment: the next time you go out for an evening, instead of scanning the room for a hookup, just for one night try to completely let go the idea. Simply enjoy the company of friends and forget about the goal of having sex, finding a boyfriend/girlfriend, etc. You will be amazed at how liberating this can be. This is not a lecture about looking for love in all the wrong places (my husband and I were introduced at a nightclub), but rather a recommendation to stop spending so much time being on the prowl that you forget to enjoy yourself and the company of your friends. Live in the moment without worrying about what happens when the nightspot closes.

I consider sex a healthy, beautiful, and divine expression of love, but it can also harm. Having sex while incapacitated by substances often leads to remorse, but can also lead to violence, disease, and unwanted pregnancy. Straight Edge people call this the poison of casual sex. So many people seek out sex as a way to fill a void, build their self-esteem, find love, etc., all of which usually leads to more bitterness and emptiness. Looking for happiness externally before finding it internally most often fails. Yoga teaches us that true happiness can only come from within. When you practice non-violence toward yourself, and see who you truly are, you will not need other people to fulfill you. Once you find this for yourself, you can enjoy less dependent and more honest relationships. You can even find many other ways to demonstrate love and intimacy besides sex, such as practicing partner yoga or offering a healing foot massage. Once you accept this, and begin to see sex in a totally different light, you can experience sex more deeply.

Personally, I interpret continence and vital energy as a moderation of sexual energy rather than as a complete abstinence. The yogic philosophy was developed exclusively for men roughly around the time when people's impressions of female deities changed. The dance celebrating the Hindu goddess Kali has radically changed, according to Dr. Ratna Roy of The Evergreen State College, an expert on classical

Indian dance. Centuries ago, women performed a feminine, graceful dance celebrating the sexual ecstasy represented by Kali. In modern India, only men can perform this dance, now full of violent and aggressive movements, emphasizing the aspect of Kali as the destroyer. Often the disparagement of sexuality is coupled with the disparagement of women. I interpret yoga philosophy from a modern feminist viewpoint. I disagree with abstaining from sex because I view the potential of sex as it was viewed in ancient times: vital, healing, spiritual, and enriching.

Instead, I interpret the retention of vital energy to mean examining my life to see where I'm wasting energy. I also find that taking immediate action helps tremendously. Instead of wasting your energy getting angry about something, confront the issue right away, and then move your brain onto another topic. If you read an article that infuriates you, immediately write a letter to the editor, and then let it go. The important thing is to take action but not to stew about an issue for days, or even years. This has been a truly difficult area for me, but I have found that by taking action right away, I can also move on to other things much faster and direct my vital energy to more healthy pursuits.

**Incorporating continence into your yoga poses:** When practicing your yoga poses, keep your brain focused on the poses to keep the vital energy of your brain in the moment. If you find yourself getting distracted, try focusing on your breath by inhaling for a count of four and exhaling for a count of four. When I find my thoughts drifting during my personal practice I will throw in a difficult balance pose, just to bring my focus back to my practice.

# Non-greed (*aparigraha*)

*Aparigraha* (ah-pah-ree-GRAH-hah)

Definition: "When non-greed is confirmed, a thorough illumination of the how and the why of one's birth comes."—*Yoga Sutras of Patanjali*, translation and commentary by Sri Swami Satchidananda

*Aparigraha* teaches us to take only what we need, and release what we do not need. Let's examine it through the lens of money. "Executive Excess 2001," a joint report by the Institute for Policy Studies and United for a Fair Economy, included a survey of 365 top United States companies. The survey showed that for companies where 1,000 or more employees lost their jobs, the Chief Executive Officers earned 80 percent more than their counterparts at other companies. I often wonder what causes someone who already has more than enough money to live comfortably to knowingly deprive others of the ability to shelter and feed their families—just to increase his own wealth. I suspect that these executives have yet to learn anything about our true nature and that they identify too closely with their powerboats and mansions. Also, based on crime statistics and quality of life studies, I have observed that capitalism breeds greed and selfishness, but more equitable economic models such as socialism breed cooperation and compassion.

Many in the punk community advocate anarchy as a societal model. While I believe it can work on a small scale, I don't think it can work on a large scale. For an anarchist society to truly be just, it would require a high degree of evolution from everyone involved—all it takes is one person who preys upon others for the system to fail. Personally, I would choose a more structured yet equitable society rather than one with more autonomy because, given the choice, I value compassion over freedom. I support the ideal of a utopian society where everyone follows their conscience and treats all others with compassion, but I believe the human race has much more evolution to accomplish before this is possible. Until that time, I believe in structured distribution of resources so that everyone can thrive.

However, no matter what societal structure people inhabit, even those of us without vast monetary wealth can still succumb to the trap of greed. No matter how much stuff we accumulate, our bodies will all meet the same final fate. We will all return into the earth and we cannot take our stuff with us. Some people view having lots of stuff as the key to immortality, which is why they buy buildings and put their names on them. But any superficial happiness that the pride of acquisition may bring lasts for only an instant, and then a new acquisition cycle must begin. This is not true happiness. However, we can all find true happiness once we stop mistakenly identifying ourselves with our stuff.

You can practice non-greed by simplifying your life. This doesn't mean selling all your furniture and eating only bread and water, but it does mean stopping to think for a moment and realize, "I have five pairs of black boots in my closet, I really do not need any more." You can certainly see a cool pair of boots and think, "Wow those are cool," and you can even buy them, provided you make room in your closet, maybe by selling other boots to a second-hand store, donating them to a charity, or giving them to a friend. But the minute you start attaching your happiness to the pair of boots—even 20-eyelet boots— you have strayed from the truth. De-cluttering takes a ton of work, but the less stuff you have, the less stuff you have to dust, so reducing your stuff gives you more free time. When you define yourself by your stuff, what happens when a fire engulfs your house? Are you destroyed? No, you are not your stuff. You are not designer clothes, sports cars, or any of that nonsense.

Certainly you can own clothing, etc., but the minute you identify yourself with a commodity, just stop and really listen to what you are saying. Even some punks, who claim to reject materialism, can fall victim to the same trap by equating their hair color, piercings, leather, and tattoos with their true identities. The minute you select your friends exclusively by what they wear, you too have fallen into this trap. Of course, this is very easy for me to say, as I have distant memories of my teenage years when identity groups were a critical part of my natural development, but I wished I had learned some of these lessons much earlier in life.

We can also examine this principle as a call to share. There's a Wiccan saying, "Whatever you send out into the world, you get back three-fold." I have experienced this three-fold concept myself. At a yoga conference I once attended, I had brought some delicious snacks and shared that food with others. A few moments later, a very gracious attendee who had rented a car for the conference offered to drive me to the airport. So, the cost of sharing my food was maybe a few dollars, but I saved a lot more by not having to take a cab. However, when we share we should do so without expecting to receive anything in return.

I will provide another example: during a bicycling trip through Washington state wine country, my husband and I both got a flat tires several miles from where we were staying and had forgotten to pack spares. A farmer tending his apple orchard offered his truck to us. He told us to "thank a Mexican kid" because the week before the only person who stopped to help him change a flat tire on a 100-degree day was a Mexican teenager. We were so grateful that we filled his gas tank and left him $50 for the trouble because it would have cost us twice that amount to get a taxi service where we were. He was not home when we returned the truck, so we left him a note instead. Later on that day, we told the story of this generous man to a winery owner—in fact we told just about anyone who would listen that day. The farmer turned out to be the winery owner's best friend. She called the farmer on the phone and we spoke—we were grateful for the opportunity to thank him by voice. Several moments later, we wrapped up at the winery and the owner told us the farmer said not to let us leave without $50 worth of wine. We protested that he was being too generous, but she said we were simply not going to win this argument with the farmer. This taught us a valuable lesson in that we need to be more like the farmer, willing to help others just because they need it, not because we want something in return. Genuine giving and sharing enlightens us and assists others, and is the best manifestation of *aparigraha*.

Sharing also means helping out and showing compassion. So, what do you do when you encounter someone asking you for money? What do you do when you suspect they will use the money to buy alcohol? Do you have to share? If you believe that money will go directly towards alcohol and you think it would cause greater harm for that person, then a better solution may be sharing some food or offering to buy a bus ticket. Or, you may give money wishing that an act of kindness could inspire someone struggling with addiction to seek help.

Personally, I prefer to donate to shelters or other programs. There is a wonderful group called Street Yoga that teaches yoga to young people who are homeless, in the foster care system, or in other crises. There are plenty of ways to share. While it seems daunting to tackle the poverty crisis in your own neighborhood, let alone around the world, you can find a way to help.

I interpret the concept of non-greed to also mean becoming a conservationist. When we look at the earth's resources as a limited quantity that we all have to share, we consider our actions differently. I challenge you to examine and improve upon your current conservation efforts. You can take some very simple steps towards reducing the amount of resources you use by riding your bike to run errands, grouping your car errands together in one trip, packing your lunch in reusable containers, cooking from scratch, eating leftovers, carpooling, taking public transportation, reducing water consumption, etc. By reducing the amount of resources you consume, you make more available for others. This also helps you practice non-violence towards the earth.

The final concept of non-greed involves emotions. Too often, we waste so much time creating our image and showing everyone around us a misrepresentation of who we really are. We attach ourselves to labels—such as goth, punk, non-smoker, vegetarian, Christian, Jew, Muslim, feminist, conservative, liberal, golfer—and not only reject everyone who does not match our narrow definition but also restrain ourselves from branching out beyond our narrow boundaries. We like our comfort zones so much that we deny other groups of people the opportunity to know us and be enriched by our presence. Try stepping outside your circle once in a while. It's truly challenging.

Even within our circles, we build walls. We say what we think others want to hear. We fear speaking our minds. We fear being ourselves because we fear rejection. This takes a lot of work, but just consider what would happen if you let your true self come through with your friends, with your family, with everyone you care about. You may find that sharing your heart with others takes less effort than hiding it.

**Incorporating non-greed into your yoga poses:** We can get really greedy with laziness, and your yoga pose practice will reflect this. If you spend most of your practice in a resting pose, such as corpse pose, you never challenge yourself. You may get attached to laziness and you will never progress. You may even regress. If you get greedy with rest, your body and mind become lethargic. On the other hand, some of us get greedy with pain, pushing ourselves beyond limits thinking, "No pain, no gain." This is nonsense—a hamstring tear makes you lose strength not gain it. As you practice your poses, observe yourself. When you find yourself spending way too much time resting, challenge yourself to push into more active poses; when you find yourself pushing to the point of injury, permit yourself to rest.

# Do something: yoga actions (*niyamas*)

The second limb of Patanjali's royal yoga involves actions (*niyamas*). The five actions were written as concisely as the five restraints—leaving us much room to analyze and interpret for ourselves.

The five actions are purity (*saucha*), contentment (*santosha*), commitment (*tapas*), spiritual study (*svadhyaya*), and surrender to the sacred (*ishvara pranidhana*). One subtle difference between the restraints and actions is that the restraints govern our interactions with others, whereas the actions tend to be more personal.

Interestingly, two of these actions seem in opposition—commitment encourages us to strive towards self-improvement, whereas contentment reminds us to celebrate who we are in the here and now. But when we remember the guideline of the middle path, we can view these as balance—and enjoy the journey as we travel forward.

The middle path also informs our interpretation of purity in that we can maintain cleanliness of body and mind without obsessing about a sterile environment.

The remaining two actions—spiritual study and surrender to the sacred—are much more personal than the other actions and restraints, as they encompass your own spirituality. My goal in articulating these tenets is not to dictate any one religious path, but rather to encourage you to examine and incorporate some form of spirituality to enrich your life.

# Purity (*saucha*)

*Saucha* (SHAUW-chah)

Definition: "By purification arises disgust for one's own body and for contact with other bodies"—*Yoga Sutras of Patanjali*, translation and commentary by Sri Swami Satchidananda

Let's consider this *niyama* in two steps: purification, and how the yogis would define "disgust" or disinterest. The yogis believe that cleanliness is not next to godliness—it is godliness. The purification concept can begin with your physical yoga practice and daily cleansing rituals, then extend into mental purification; it includes mind, body, and living space. If your body and the space in which you practice yoga poses and meditation are not clean, that makes it all the more difficult to cleanse the mind. In a rough example, you cannot really meditate with five cups of coffee coursing through your system.

Some yogis will insist that your yoga practice space consist solely of a mat, and perhaps a blanket. In the *Hatha Yoga Pradipika*, we are instructed to cleanse the walls of our space with cow dung to fight disease (keep in mind when this was written). Modern yoga studios invest quite a bit in lighting, airflow, wall color, etc. If you can afford to practice in a studio and have found a studio where you feel comfortable, wonderful. But many people cannot afford to practice in a studio every day, so they practice at home. It would be equally wonderful if we could all own a home that has a studio room just for yoga, but many of us practice where we can—living rooms, bedrooms, parks, and beaches.

So, we make compromises in the color of the walls and amount of daylight, but here's some simple things you really need to do: 1) vacuum or sweep often so you're not stepping on crumbs; 2) open a window for some fresh air; 3) clear out a decent amount of space for you to practice so that you do not smack a hand or foot— even if you have to temporarily pile a bunch of things on the couch or bed; 4) cover your books, computers, and paperwork so you are not distracted by any work—fabric store remnants work wonderfully for these things.

In addition to a clean space, yogis have lots of theories on a clean body. Many yoga instructors advocate taking a bath or shower before practicing the poses or meditating. Water is the essence of purification in many religious and cultural practices. In India, many practice some intense cleansing rituals. The *Hatha Yoga Pradipika* describes extensive cleansing rituals of every bodily orifice (while I find the use of a neti pot invaluable, I stop short of some of the more intense enema practices). The neti pot—filled with warm salty water and designed to cleanse nasal passages—has crossed over into mainstream Western use. If you suffer from allergies or constant congestion, this can help tremendously. Saunas and steam rooms also work wonders with the nasal passages, along with purifying the skin. Many of the purification rituals make sense in this context: sinus congestion makes breath work grueling. So, even by placing your face a few inches over a cup of boiling water and inhaling steam or taking a hot shower with eucalyptus soap may make all the difference in your breathing.

In addition to external cleaning, purity refers to what we eat, drink, inhale, and inject. Drugs of any form in excess—even caffeine—make the physical and meditative practices of yoga difficult. The more yoga you do, the more you can feel happy naturally, so ultimately you can reduce most drug dependency. When you discover the impermanent nature of what we consider reality, you may not feel compelled to escape it with drugs. Yoga alone is no cure for heroin addiction, but it definitely can help with the rehabilitation process. Henry Rollins said it best when he said, "Keep your blood clean, your body lean, and your mind sharp."

Except for certain drugs like heroin or crack, which are insidiously addictive, we also have the concept of moderation. Some people can consume alcohol in moderation, and some research supports it as healthy, but all researchers conclude that excessive consumption is harmful. Coffee, green tea, and black tea have powerful healing effects—particularly for the liver—however, the minute you feel the addiction, as when you cannot make it through a single lazy Sunday without caffeine, you know you need to honestly examine your consumption. Also, I want to clarify some misconceptions I've come across in my travels: zoning out while stoned is not liberation. Marijuana does not bring you true liberation—despite whatever temporary feelings it may bring.

Beyond the obvious chemicals, you should also examine your diet. If we are what we eat, some of us are pretty messed up. In the yogic philosophy, food is sacred, healing, and sustaining. For one week, try examining your food through the lens of what it contributes, such as a sweet potato giving you beta-carotene, which helps your eyesight.

If you keep a journal of all that you eat and the benefits it gives you, you can change your perspective on eating completely. Of course we need proteins and fats, but we do not need monosodium glutamate, high-fructose corn syrup, or partially-hydrogenated anything. The macrobiotic movement advocates eating food as close to its original source as possible; barbeque-flavored potato chips are pretty far removed. Certainly, it's fine to have some chocolate (which in a dark form actually benefits the body) or junk food every once in a while, but the healthier the diet and the fewer chemicals we consume through food the better. It takes time, but you should start reading labels and become aware of what you ingest. Try a week of eliminating all processed foods, then another week eliminating alcohol, and another eliminating caffeine, etc. and notice the effects.

When hepatitis nearly destroyed my body, I read everything I could about it and divided things into two groups: hurt the liver, and heal the liver. I lived on flax, soy, leafy vegetables, and protein shakes, and avoided alcohol, kava, acetaminophen, and many food additives. I drank as much green tea and red tea as I could. When you eat consciously, considering everything you eat as nourishing and providing your body with vital elements, you can develop a much more healthy relationship with food. This healthy, healing relationship with food not only can reduce our obsession with food, it also can cleanse the body.

Once we have purified the body, we can work deeper on purifying the mind. Some advocate eliminating all negative images and sounds from your life. While some interpret this to mean never watching the news, I take a less extreme position and advocate eliminating violent recreation such as most video games. Researchers have found that playing violent video games increases violent behavior both in the short term—while playing the game—and in the long term. Video games, television, movies, etc. all provide a form of escape, so first you have to ask yourself, "From what am I escaping?" By trying to answer that question, you are taking the very critical first step towards purification. Another step, and perhaps an easier one, is to mind your emotions before and after viewing violent imagery. Take stock of your heart rate, your muscle tension, and your thoughts before watching a program you typically watch, then scan yourself again after. Your body will tell you very clearly that the violent imagery affects you.

Some people never read or watch the news because they want to purify themselves of all the violence and hatred in the world. I think this is great to do every so often. If you cannot go camping or go on a retreat at least once a year, then try to do mini-retreats. Try for a weekend to not watch television, read the newspaper, or listen to the radio and avoid all forms of advertising. Retreats are wonderful and help you renew. However if you always ignore the world around you and ignore the suffering of others by not staying informed, voting, or taking other actions to help prevent violence, then you are violating the principle of non-violence. If you choose to lead a monastic life, that's one thing, but if you participate in the world, you should do so mindfully so you can have a positive impact. For example, it might be fun to purchase cute little yoga tops, but not if the manufacturer has abusive labor practices. If you live in the world, you should know something about it, but you can choose your news sources wisely as well; if you listen to people screaming on talk radio, you may struggle with a sense of peace. Every once in a while, you need to dial it down and balance the aggressive sensory input.

Even though we can reduce the sensory input, the physical world presents numerous stressors. While we work to transcend the more animalistic tendencies, we first must acknowledge our basic biology. In yogic philosophy, three elements called *gunas* rule our physical and emotional selves. We will discuss the *gunas* further in the chapter, "Unmask the aspects of nature (*gunas*) and face your character (*dosha*)." In a nutshell, *rajas* is aggressive, hyperactive, and fiery; *tamas* is passive, sluggish, and cold; *sattva* is the middle one: pure, peaceful, and balanced. Clinical psychologists might diagnose someone with excessive *rajas* as having attention-deficit disorder and someone with excessive *tamas* as being depressed. In yoga, we seek to balance *rajas* and *tamas* and bring ourselves into a state of *sattva* and then, ultimately, liberate ourselves from the three states completely.

At any given time, one of these states could dominate, so we need balance. I'll put this in terms of music: if you only listen to digital hardcore, then the state of aggression will squash the others, but if you feel depressed, unmotivated, and sluggish, then emo music will drag you further down. Ultimately, we want to transcend the aggression and sullenness, but first we must acknowledge it. I like to imagine using my inner fire (*tapas*) as a way to burn through these states of extremes—unleashing a primary scream or shedding tears. Harmless release rather than suppression moves us along the awareness path towards liberation. The faster we can acknowledge the extremes, and trace their triggers, the faster we can transcend them.

The final concept of purity involves disinterest with your own body and with others. Yogis believe that once you view the body as always unclean—just imagine the amount of bacteria on your tongue—you will be disinterested by both your own body and by the bodies of others. This viewpoint clashes with my personal views on the earth as sacred and soil as a live-giving force. Keep in mind that yogic philosophy is subject to individual interpretation—only you know what is really sacred and what is not.

A better way to view this concept involves regarding the body as constantly changing, never in a pure state, so we should regard the body as just an ever-changing vehicle. Of course, the plastic surgery industry would crumble if everyone suddenly embraced this concept, but the point is to not associate yourself with what you see in the mirror. This is not an excuse for not bathing or grooming—in fact, *saucha* insists on cleanliness—but rather a directive to not obsess over your appearance. In other words, keep your face clean, but if you get a zit, accept it, clean it, and do not let it define you.

**Incorporating purity into your yoga poses:** During a vigorous practice, you will sweat, especially if you practice in a heated room. By showering quickly before your practice, you will remove surface dirt, allowing your pores to release the sweat. At a minimum, make sure you remove makeup before practicing so your face can breathe. Flushing the body with plenty of water before and after a vigorous practice further aids the internal cleansing of the body that we do during a yoga practice. In addition to cleansing the body, keep your practice space clean. If you use a yoga mat, soak it in the bathtub or in direct sunlight once a month to cleanse it.

# Contentment (*santosha*)

*Santosha* (san-TOE-shah)

Definition: "By contentment, supreme joy is gained."—*Yoga Sutras of Patanjali*, translation and commentary by Sri Swami Satchidananda

This wonderful guideline instructs us to be happy right here and now. What could be simpler? But of course, *santosha* is not that simple. This guideline does not tell us to sit on our bottom all day, but instead instructs us to do our best, and rejoice in putting our best effort forward, regardless of the final results. This also teaches us to live in the moment, without worrying about the future and regretting the past. Too often, we preface our statements with "if," as in, "If I only had a million dollars, I could be happy. If I were thinner, taller, prettier, stronger, smarter, etc." One way I practice this concept is to tell myself "I would like to make enough money to provide for my son and maybe someday spend a year sailing the world." But the real work is to say, "I will be happy with where I am here and now. I will find a way to be happy every day."

You should set goals, keep learning, and keep growing, but also recognize there is no shame in where you are right now. The yogis tell us to take pride in every job we do. Certainly musicians, actors, professional athletes, and corporate executives make lots of money, but the heroic mythology some societies have cultivated towards them is baseless. There is dignity in every honest job. Everyone should take pride in the honest contributions they make. The original skinhead movement in 1960s London—which espoused inter-racial harmony— embraced the concept of hard work: work hard, live clean, be proud of who you are, and don't take crap from the ruling class. The movement demonstrated that manual labor jobs have as much honor and dignity as white-collar jobs. Fancy houses do not bring happiness; true happiness comes from the inside. Without indulging in schadenfreude, one only needs to read a celebrity magazine once to realize that liberation and financial wealth are often at odds.

Again, the magic word moderation rears its head; we should set goals and work toward those goals, but throughout the process, celebrate each step along the way. In many Western societies, we define life in terms of point "A" and point "B." We see ourselves at the start and want to get to the end. Yoga teaches us to savor the nectar in the continuum—the lessons we learn along the way are where the juice is.

We can demonstrate this in terms of yoga postures. If you work for years trying to do an advanced pose, you learn so much about yourself. You examine your fears, your resistance, and every obstacle you encounter while working into the pose. But, if you can do an advanced pose right away, you learn absolutely nothing about yourself other than you can perform, say, a handstand. Too often we do the poses that come easily to us, but instead we should do the poses that challenge us the most and every time we do them, we should take note and think, "I am thrilled that I have made it this far in the pose. I'll stay here a while and reflect on what I have learned so far. Maybe tomorrow I can learn something new about myself when I try it again."

One question I constantly ask myself is: "Am I living the CliffsNotes version of my life or am I truly exploring?" When you watch a movie, do you fast-forward to the end just to know the ending? Usually we do not because we want to empathize with the characters and enjoy the entire plot development. Yet in our lives, we too often hit the fast-forward button, skipping all of the good stuff in the middle. We begin semesters at school by counting the days until the next break. We jump into bed with people so quickly that we know very little about them first, which makes the sex a far poorer experience. We long for the weekend so desperately that we lack joy in our workweek. Sadly, education in the U.S. encourages this behavior—the culture of testing means teachers focus so heavily on a single end result that the process of learning gets ignored.

The first step is to recognize this pattern in your life, and the next step is to change it, which is not easy. It's challenging to practice contentment while working at a job where you have completed your tasks for the day but are still obligated to sit at a desk until a certain time. However, through practicing other principles, such as honesty, you may find ways to fill out the rest of your day by taking on additional tasks, or you could try to negotiate to bring a book or leave early for your lighter days. I realize that corporate culture often leaves little room for this type of honest behavior, but it's critical to stop living your life in the future by thinking, "Once my work day is over, then I can be happy." It's important to find happiness even in what we consider mundane.

Having a child has pushed me into more contentment. Staying home to raise a child transformed my life into a simpler one—more manual work such as laundry and diapering, and less conceptual work such as, say, designing data models. But along with the more routine tasks comes great joy, especially on rough days where I celebrate the fact that the laundry managed to get cleaned. Also, young children see the world with such an infectious wonder that you have no choice but to begin marveling at the patterns of woodchips and pondering the lives of scurrying ants.

Another aspect of childrearing, unfortunately, is the hyper-competitiveness. There are charts to track everything, and with those charts come nervous, insecure parents who constantly want their child to measure-up. I have had to truly practice contentment with my child's accomplishments as they come, and ignore the quantitative milestones such as how many words children should be articulating at certain ages. Letting go of competition and celebrating my child as he is each moment has been a wonderful challenge to me to deepen my practice of contentment. I am sure that in your life you can find some equivalent of letting go, slowing down, and enjoying the present moment.

**Incorporating contentment into your yoga poses:** So much about yoga teaches us contentment, permitting yourself to enjoy the here and now, and take pride in your accomplishments along the way. Yoga is practice, not perfection. There is no graduation in yoga; even when you have "mastered" a pose you can further challenge yourself by adding a new arm option, closing your eyes, lengthening the breath, staying in the pose longer, etc. Every time you practice a pose, tell yourself, "I am getting stronger every time," or "I am building flexibility every time," and stop worrying about looking like an acrobat. Someday, you may be able to put your foot behind your head, but if you never do that, so what? The poses teach us about ourselves and they teach us to savor every moment. Every time we take a breath, we can feel grateful for being alive. As you practice your poses, cultivate joie de vivre. If you take the time to savor each pose, and celebrate the accomplishments you have made with each pose, you will find yourself savoring more of life.

# Commitment (*tapas*)

*Tapas* (TAH-pahs)

Definition: "By austerity, impurities of the body and senses are destroyed and occult powers gained."—*Yoga Sutras of Patanjali*, translation and commentary by Sri Swami Satchidananda

Yogis define occult powers as the ability to see the impermanence of the physical and emotional world and the ability to become one with universal and eternal truth. This has nothing to do with sorcery per se, but instead addresses the true nature of life, not the superficial manifestations we see, touch, and feel. Regardless of your perspective on the true nature of reality, you can appreciate the rigorous commitment to seek the truth through meditation, much like the dedication scientists demonstrate in their quests.

*Tapas* literally means to burn, so this tenet instructs us to burn off all that stands in our way of uniting ourselves with our true self. This includes our attachments to our bodies, our emotions, and our stuff. Burning is cathartic, as seen in events such as the Burning Man festival, where the art is ultimately burned and destroyed, thus symbolizing the impermanence of all that we see, and the liberation we feel when we burn our attachments to objects. By following this yogic principle of commitment, we stand up, face our demons, and commit to conquering them. This teaches us to face reality straight in the eye, see it for what it truly is, burn through all our physical and emotional problems associated with reality, then finally liberate ourselves from day-to-day reality. We learn that what we think is real is not really real. How real is advertising? That's not the true nature of things. When we persevere to focus within, we see the truth.

Yogis also interpret this principle as commitment, will power, and dedication. We can think of this as the fuel for our yoga practice. Too often, we quit over minor obstructions. In yoga, we may encounter a difficult pose and give up; in life, we abandon things when they get rough. You can, of course, realize that you're on the wrong path, such as having a job that you find morally objectionable, and quit. That's very different from giving up when you encounter difficulties. Note that in yoga we see numerous paths all leading to the same destination: liberation. Sometimes we deviate from the path, but we can jump right back on the path and pick up where we left off. We can fall off the path in many ways—usually addictions to various things (drugs, money, power, materialism, food, etc.). Anything that anesthetizes, stupefies, or distracts us stops us in our tracks. Yes, one limb of yoga involves withdrawing from the senses, but that involves action. When you get stoned and tune out, you passively allow a chemical to take over your sensory abilities and that's not yoga. Many define yoga as a mental discipline, emphasizing the word discipline. You can certainly watch television and have sex and enjoy a glass of wine, but when those pursuits start taking over, and you make no time for any introspective pursuits, then you need some discipline and some fire.

So many of us seek distractions to escape our reality. We could spend the whole book discussing the "every man for himself" societal norms that makes us feel lonely, isolated, and paranoid. I have no use for the culture of fear highlighted on the evening news or the advertising bombardment that constantly berates us—"You too could be happy, if you only get your teeth whitened!" Modern living smacks us with lots of reasons to drop out and escape, but normal means of escape are just temporary. Some people describe the secret to happiness as alcohol and television, but once the buzz wears off and the program ends only a headache and exhaustion remain. Escape is not liberation. While I advocate repairing society, I believe in fixing ourselves as well. The more people who stop dropping out and start kicking in the better off we all will be.

So, what happens if you slip off the path and slip into, say, a heroin addiction or an unhealthy relationship? According to yogic philosophy, you can hop back on the path exactly where you left off. Let's delve into an Indian belief that may or may not jive with your beliefs, but one that you can interpret on several levels. Many yoga practitioners believe in reincarnation, and that you will go through a cycle of rebirths until you have balanced or exhausted your *karma* (consequences of your actions). As long as you have *tapas*, or the fire to see the truth, you can even continue on your work from one lifetime to the next. If the concept of multiple lifetimes does not match your belief system, you can think of reincarnation as life cycles within your lifetime—such as Maiden-Mother-Crone, Boy-Father-Elder—or you can even think of it as our hormonal cycles. Interpret this concept from your heart and find what makes the most sense to you. The Indigo Girls in their song "Galileo" brilliantly explained the cycle of rebirth as our spirit gets closer and closer to ultimate wisdom. (I know the Indigo Girls are not punk, but lighten up.)

Oddly enough, the principle I have struggled to commit to is commitment. In fact, this book has been several years in the making. A huge challenge with commitment is our fear of choosing the wrong option. Fear of getting it wrong paralyzes many of us into inertia. People like to keep their options open sometimes way too often. Socially, too many people respond to invitations with a "maybe" instead of a "yes" because they are waiting to see if something better comes up, not because they feel an illness coming on. As I see how people use technology these days, I see so many people just dipping one toe into life—being physically with one group of people, but chatting on the phone and texting with others. Fear of missing out on something better keeps us from living in the present moment.

One way to view commitment is to distinguish between committing to our eternal self rather than our impermanent self. Something inside of us transcends parties, concerts, and other events and acknowledging that makes it much easier to accept going to or missing out on an event. Lots of people struggle to choose a major in college, decide on a place to live, a career path, etc. Aside from being an assassin or a predatory financier, very few jobs are truly wrong. I believe that a lack of introspection and meditation causes commitment-phobia. Take the time to self-study, choose a direction, and then commit to it. Keep in mind the impermanence of everything external so that even if you find yourself traveling on the wrong highway, you can change direction. But once you find yourself changing direction more often than some people change the television channel, stop and commit to a meditative practice so you can find the right path for you.

**Incorporating commitment into your yoga poses:** Some people practice in hot rooms to add fire to their practice. Yoga poses work best in a warm environment, so that you have adequate relaxation of the muscles. However, I recommend that you focus on the fire of commitment in your practice. The hardest part about a yoga pose practice is starting. Make a firm schedule for yourself by first committing to practicing once a week for an hour, or by committing a few minutes a day. Write it down and stick to it. Set a reminder so that you will stick with it. Perhaps even enlist the help of a true friend. Make a promise to yourself that you will practice every day. Then, in your practice, keep the fire burning. Imagine yourself fueling a giant fire inside that burns off all the emotional and chemical crap you no longer need. Fuel the fire with strong breath. And when you hit a plateau, find a new challenge in yoga—attempting a new pose, practicing with your eyes closed, studying a different style, etc. Keep growing with your practice and keep the fire alive.

# Spiritual study (*svadhyaya*)

*Svadhyaya* (swahd-YAH-yah)

Definition: "By study of spiritual books comes communion with one's deity."—*Yoga Sutras of Patanjali,* translation and commentary by Sri Swami Satchidananda

This practice involves studying spiritual information. I extend this information to include not just books but also story-telling, art, music, poetry, and dance. Anything that provides you insight, wisdom, and connects you to a higher truth is a spiritual resource.

The problem, of course, happens when people fight about what is spiritual and what is not. Men have fought countless wars arguing, "My god is better than your god." I find this insane. Gandhi said that he was a Hindu and a Muslim and a Christian and a Jew because he saw all the world's religions ultimately converging on the same thing. When I examine the origins of Islam, Judaism, and Christianity, and I see the similarities amongst them, I scratch my head trying to figure out what war has to do with God.

The yogic standpoint on God is: God will manifest itself to you in the way that is most sacred to you. This echoes in the Bahá'í faith, which says that all religions of the world are worshipping the same God, but with different rituals. In fact, within the Bahá'í faith, you can continue to worship as a Catholic, Muslim, or a shaman and still consider yourself Bahá'í. Bahá'í has a social counterpart, which advocates racial, gender and socio-economic equality. One often-used Bahá'í parable calls men and women the two wings of the bird of humanity. The bird can only fly when both wings are equally strong. (As disclosure, I do not identify myself as a Bahá'í, but I deeply respect its principles.)

We must begin by fully examining what we consider sacred. Very few of us actually do so in our lives. I was raised Catholic, but have explored numerous other belief systems and consider myself a bit of a buffet spiritualist, loading aspects from many beliefs onto my plate. However, my foundational Catholic beliefs stuck with me until I had a miscarriage.

After my miscarriage I became spiritually lost. Everything I ever believed was suddenly a lie. Why would God create a baby just to have it die in the womb? That was unintelligent design to me. I wanted to tell Brian Greene just where he could stick his "elegant universe." At the time, I was reading some classic yoga philosophy and tossed the books aside more than once, considering it all nonsense.

But then the healing process began and with it came time for reflection—forced reflection in fact. In trying to reconcile my emotional pain with my beliefs I realized two primary components: one is that believing in something sacred is no talisman that will protect you from having any sort of misfortune, and secondly that the lessons of yoga do help us make sense of the world. My experience reminded me that our attachments to our expectations are a true source of pain, and that contentment is critical—instead of mourning what could have been, we should celebrate what is here and now. Of course, we must find the middle path between celebrating what we have and becoming overly attached, but there is a middle path in there somewhere.

Though this had not been the first time I questioned my beliefs, it was the first time I had them totally shaken. While I never wish anyone to undergo a pain such as miscarriage, I believe everyone should seriously spend time pondering the existence of some sort of spiritual force.

While some groups within organized religions encourage scrutinizing beliefs, most discourage it—in fact if a Muslim leaves the faith they become an apostate, which is punishable by death according to sharia law. While Christians and members of other religious groups may not face that horrible fate, most people, out of fear, never seriously question their religious teachings. I believe that if more people seriously examined their faith and tried to answer for themselves whether or not they truly believe in God, then they would feel far more confident in their beliefs and far less likely to feel threatened by the beliefs of others.

On the other side, of course, are atheists and I believe fear prevents many of them from spending introspective time exploring the possibility of a spiritual force. It's easy to walk around quoting Nietzsche with a sneer ("God is dead.") but it's not so easy to examine whether or not you believe that to be true. I have heard scientists say that the existence of God is an unanswerable question and therefore not intellectually interesting. While I agree they have their own worthy scientific pursuits, I find it puzzling that many of these intellectuals have never once stopped to contemplate whether there is a higher purpose to our existence. I do know some people who have pondered this very deeply and concluded they do not believe in a higher power—

and that is completely valid; the important thing is to study, meditate, and examine.

I would love to tell you I have definitive proof of God's existence, but that would be a lie. You need to answer this for yourself, but also allow that you may spend a tremendous amount of time in the questioning stage. Questioning and contemplating are steps on the yogic path.

While many people have subverted religion for political and economic gain, you should explore lessons from people you consider spiritual—and note that even atheists can be spiritual. Once you explore those lessons, try to make sense of them for yourself and apply them to your life. As you read things that resonate with you, write them down, make notes, meditate on it, and compare it to other things you have read.

Ultimately, you define spirituality for yourself, but have some common sense. You can read the *Bible*, the *Tibetan Book of the Dead*, *The Upanishads*, etc. You can also read modern popular philosophers such as Deepak Chopra, Maya Angelou, and Henry Rollins. You can reach back further to movements such as the transcendentalists and read Ralph Waldo Emerson. In fact, you should study numerous philosophers for insight. Even certain movies can be sacred. Think about what you read, see, and hear. Does it make you think or make you numb? Does it lift you up or drag you down? While I have no right telling you what is sacred and not sacred, I trust that if you examine your literature honestly you will find certain things have a gift of wisdom and others certainly do not. Keep an open mind. Read, hear, and see lots, then find something that resonates with you and study it exhaustively.

Alternatively, many people find spirituality outside of human creations. Communing with nature may sound like a hippie cliché, but immersing yourself in the ocean, scrambling up a mountain, or just simply gazing at a river can profoundly impact your worldview, not to mention your serenity. You can contemplate the magnitude and forces surrounding you, or simply allow the sensory input of nature to wash away your racing thoughts. This does not mean you have to trek to Patagonia, as wonderful as that sounds. Every city has some green spot—look past the cigarette butts and other flotsam and find something majestic around you, even if it's as simple as a single leaf.

**Incorporating spiritual study into your yoga poses:** To take your poses to another level, begin each practice by reading a profound passage from a spiritual work, focusing on a spiritual piece of art, or listening to some spiritual music. As you practice the poses, chant a word or a phrase from the spiritual work. Imagine that each pose helps you fully absorb the profound word or phrase from your reading/listening/viewing. You can use a book like *The Yoga Sutras of Patanjali*, texts from your religion, poetry, etc. Or, you can truly do it yourself: at the end of one practice session, take a few minutes to compose your own spiritual song, chant, or poem and then incorporate that into your next practice. Be your own spiritual reference.

# Surrender to the sacred (*ishvara pranidhana*)

*Ishvara pranidhana* (eesh-VAR-ah prah-nee-DAH-nah)

Definition: "By total surrender to God, samadhi is obtained."—*Yoga Sutras of Patanjali*, translation and commentary by Sri Swami Satchidananda

Here's where yoga gets kind of fuzzy. Repeat after me: "Yoga is not a religion, but a mental discipline." It does, ultimately, deepen your connection with your religious beliefs and brings you closer to a union with what you consider sacred. That union brings you liberation.

This concept often creates confusion and misconceptions about yoga. Some religious leaders denounce yoga as devil worship. This sounds ridiculous, of course, but there is a prevailing thought in some circles that meditation opens your mind to the devil, despite the history of meditation in those very religions. Even the Bible recommends meditation: "This book of the law shall not depart out of thy mouth; but thou shall meditate therein day and night…"—Joshua Chapter 1, Verse 8.

Yoga's ties to Hinduism create confusion and some yoga teachers do little to clarify the distinction. Yoga and Hinduism evolved in the same place, and they share some philosophical lineages. But yoga does not assume Hinduism and not all Hindus practice yoga. Yoga does assume that you have some sense of a higher power, but this higher power does not have to be Shiva, nor does it have to be any anthropomorphized view of God, nor does a higher power have to mean an omnipotent controller. For many yoga practitioners, the sacred, or the higher power, is a universal, eternal force that illuminates all of us, and others describe it as a continual vibration that resonates within each one of us. If those definitions sound too "woo-woo" for you, that's fine, but contemplate on what you find sacred, and find something inside yourself that connects you with your view of the sacred. We all have a sense that something transcends our daily existence and worries.

Surrender to the sacred means complete devotion to what you consider sacred. I consider this the cumulative principle, because if you are practicing all the other restraints and actions diligently, you essentially have surrendered to the sacred. This tenet calls for more introspection and personal interpretation than the other nine, because you have to define the concept of sacred. Even atheists can consider something sacred, so they will define it in their own way. Many Native Americans consider the earth sacred, and devote their lives to respecting and caring for the earth.

To better understand it, let's also look at what surrender to the sacred is not. It is not war, it is not hatred, it is not prejudice, it is not destruction, and it is not violence. Surrendering to the sacred does not necessarily mean abdicating your duties or withdrawing from the world.

Sri Swami Satchidananda summarized it best when he said, "Be good. Do good." You might be wondering, how can something so simple become so complex? Why do people wage war in the name of what they consider sacred? I think people who wage war in the name of their god have a false sense of surrender and an attachment to their ego—they believe their family will be rewarded and they will receive rewards in an afterlife. This is selfishness, not surrender.

Here's how I interpret this principle personally. To me, God manifests in the love I share with my family. That love is my sacred. I aspire to have an unselfish devotion to my family. For me, truly loving someone has been the most liberating element of my entire life. I thought I had understood the depths of devotion when I married, but having a child showed me a level of devotion I never conceived possible. I surrender to the sacred by devoting myself to my family. Some may say that I have not renounced my attachment to my family, and therefore I am not completely surrendering to a higher power. I have heard that argument and understand its basis, but we all interpret the sacred in the way most meaningful to us. No matter how you interpret it, by truly devoting yourself to what you consider sacred, you will liberate yourself.

A huge complexity of yoga is that it calls for us to renounce our attachments to everything–even our attachment to the idea of the sacred. This will sound strange, but by letting go of all your attachments, fully surrendering to what you consider to be sacred, and then finally letting go of your attachment to that, then you will find yourself truly liberated. But, take this one step at a time; most of us will spend our lives just trying to surrender to our concept of the sacred.

One elegant way to think about surrendering to the sacred is through acts of compassion. When Malcolm X visited Mecca, he heard a principle of surrender that would forever change his outlook. Dr.

Mahmoud Youssef Shawarbi told him, "No man has believed perfectly until he wishes for his brother what he wishes for himself."

**Incorporating surrender to the sacred into your yoga poses:** Several of my favorite teachers have a fabulous way of incorporating this concept into their classes. At the beginning of your practice session, think about someone out there that needs some extra strength. At the beginning of your session, dedicate the strength you generate in each pose to that person. In every pose, remind yourself of the dedication, and imagine yourself sending your strength out to your beneficiary. Now, there's no scientific study showing that standing strong in a warrior pose will help your grandmother fight cancer, but it will deepen your practice and deepen your love for someone else. The more you can love others, the stronger your connection to what you consider sacred.

# Strike a pose (*asana*)

In the *Yoga Sutras of Patanjali*, you will find one sentence about poses: "You should take a comfortable seat." That's it. So, how did we get from one sentence describing a comfortable meditative posture to a myriad of yoga pose classes? The *Hatha Yoga Pradipika* played a major role. In this later work, practitioners advocated that starting with the behavioral elements of the *yoga sutras* set aspiring yogis up for failure, and that before a person can purge their mental demons they must first purge their physical demons. Hence, in this work, Swami Swatmarama describes poses, breathing exercises, and cleansing techniques. This work evolved into the myriad of yoga pose classes we see today. All of the pose classes stem from some form of hatha yoga.

The goal of the pose practice in yoga is two-fold. The first is to cleanse the body of all waste products resulting in aches and pains so that the body can sit peacefully in meditation for a long time. The second is to unite two complimentary energies believed to dwell in each of us: an aggressive, fiery, masculine energy of the sun (*ha*), and a receptive, cool, feminine energy of the moon (*tha*). The belief is that our feminine energy is coiled at the base of our spine like a serpent, and once we remove all our physical and mental barriers to liberation, this energy rises up to join with our masculine energy at the crown of our head. Only when we unite these two forces can we truly experience liberation. The practice of kundalini yoga is focused solely on this action.

Note that you do not have to follow Hinduism, nor do you have to believe that you literally have a serpentine energy at the base of your spine, to benefit from this philosophy. The idea of masculine and feminine energy is hardly unique to yoga. In Chinese philosophy it is called yang and yin. In examining your daily interactions you notice that knowing when to be assertive and when to step back and listen is a huge asset. My brief experience in motherhood so far has taught me there are definite times for asserting my authority, and definite times for patiently listening. By practicing a balance of both energizing and calming poses in yoga, I do believe that we can achieve a greater balance in our aggressive and receptive natures.

Also, in the West, we use the poses as physical therapy—healing and strengthening our muscles and joints. Purists may say that practicing poses merely for physical benefits misses the point of yoga. I say, so what! Sure, it's not Yoga with a capital "Y," but the poses and pose sequences found in yoga have extraordinary benefits as a balanced strength and flexibility regimen and as an antidote for the havoc wreaked by bodies being slumped over computers for hours.

Not that I am ruling out writing one someday, but yoga pose books and videos abound, and I wanted to focus on the philosophy of yoga. Also, I strongly believe in working with a teacher when beginning a yoga pose practice because misalignment in poses can hurt the body.

So instead of presenting you with specific poses, I will articulate some of the ways in which you can use yoga poses for therapy, provide tips on balancing your own home practice, and shed some light on the various yoga pose class styles so you can find the right teacher and style for you. If you have not taken a yoga class yet, please do not be intimidated by the pose names—there are videos all over the internet that will illustrate these clearly to you. Or—even better—you can take a class and ask your teacher.

Yoga poses have different effects on us mentally and physically. Backbends such as cobra (*bhujangasana*) tend to awaken us, while forward bends such as standing forward fold (*uttanasana*) tend to calm us. Balance poses such as dancer (*natarajasana*) help us focus. Rhythmic flowing from one pose to the next, as found in classic yoga pose sequences such as sun salutations (*surya namaskara*), has a meditative effect, particularly because of the rhythmic breathing. (While steady, rhythmic breathing should be practiced in all yoga poses, flowing pose sequences effectively keep people focused on rhythmic breathing.) I have found both as a teacher and as a student that inversion, or upside-down, poses have a mixed effect on people—once you have practiced inversions diligently for several months they can be calming, but until then inversions can cause an adrenaline rush. Some poses require great muscle endurance, which fuels our aggressive side, while others allow us to relax without using our muscles for support, which fuels our receptive side.

You will find that the more you practice poses at home, and pay attention to your mental state and energy level before and after attending classes, the more you can attune your home practice to meet your psychological and physical needs. For example, after a stressful day, I often like to focus on more relaxing poses; however, if I start with those, my nervous energy will make my whole body twitch. So I start with some sun salutations and one or two poses I find physically challenging in order to burn off the aggressive fire, and then move into more calming, cooling poses and make that the bulk of my practice.

Eventually you will reach this state where you intuitively know what poses you need to practice, but it truly helps to start with a class and a good teacher.

Differentiating among the various names for yoga classes often prevents or at least delays new students from practicing. Vinyasa? Yin? Astanga? Iyengar? Punk Rock Yoga? What?! I'll highlight a few of the predominant styles and discuss my own.

As I mentioned earlier, all the yoga pose class styles originate from *hatha*, and some simply call their classes hatha yoga. Other styles are named for the creators, such as Iyengar yoga, which focuses on holding poses for a long time and achieving perfect alignment (often using props for support), and Bikram yoga, which consists of 26 poses performed in a hot room in the exact same order with the teachers saying the exact same thing every time.

Another style, astanga yoga, often confuses people because the *Yoga Sutras of Patanjali* is referred to as *astanga*, which means eight limbs. While astanga yoga teachers certainly study the eight-limb philosophy, the classes involve flowing from pose to pose with the breath, following well-defined sequences. Another form of flowing yoga is called vinyasa, which means flow, but in this style teachers are more likely to improvise the traditional sequences from astanga yoga and create their own.

Kundalini yoga classes involve extensive breathing exercises with a strong focus on the theory of uniting feminine and masculine energy. In a yin yoga class, students hold passive poses for extended periods of time—at least five minutes—emphasizing stretching connective tissue. In a Viniyoga class, teachers emphasize adapting poses to match the physical needs and limitations of their students.

There are numerous other styles out there. While some styles might seem very similar, other styles have distinctly different philosophies and focus.

Before joining a class, ask the teacher directly about the content and direction of the class. I would say to beware of teachers and styles that claim they teach the only "authentic" yoga. (If we go back to the origins of yoga and want to be technical about it, authentic yoga would be restricted to men only.) Avoid those who get hung up on the trivia. The right class and teacher for you will leave your body invigorated yet relaxed and your spirit intrigued yet elevated.

I recommend taking various classes and then finding the style that works best for you. High-change people may find yin yoga tedious and low-change people may find vinyasa yoga intimidating. But, on the other hand, the hyperactive person may find yin yoga a healthy way to slow down and the sluggish person may find vinyasa yoga a great way to boost energy. I also recommend trying to incorporate different styles within your practice—for example, practicing flowing, more energetic yoga on some days, while doing a more restorative, yin-style practice on others. For a home practice, structure it by moving the spine in four ways: forward as in downward facing dog (*adho mukha svanasana*), backward as in upward facing dog (*urdhva mukha svanasana*), side-to-side as in triangle (*trikonasna*), and twisting as in half lord of the fishes (*ardha matseyandrasana*).

So, what about Punk Rock Yoga classes? Most teachers use a flowing style, but they also add lots of uniqueness to their classes. Some of the main distinctions involve the atmosphere of the class. Punk Rock Yoga teachers approach their classes with the humility that they are sharing the practice with the students, and they avoid behaving like, well, rock stars. Classes usually set up in a circle, so the teacher is on the same plane as the students and the students do not self-rank. Lights dim to avoid staring at others competitively. Live music often finds its way into the class, keeping students engaged in the practice while providing a wonderful creative challenge for musicians as well. Students are encouraged to think for themselves and sometimes create their own yoga flows. Also, much of the philosophy you have read in this book is presented to students with a frank, yet open-minded approach by the teacher.

Finding a yoga teacher who meshes with you will keep you practicing. It may take some time, and it may mean practicing with videos for a while until you find the right teacher. Even though yoga emphasizes individual responsibility and you have the right to opt out or modify every pose in the class, you still want to find teachers who know what they are doing.

Don't be afraid to ask for a teacher's credentials. There are numerous training organizations and an umbrella organization called the Yoga Alliance that provides a list of registered teachers—which means they accumulated either 200 or 500 training hours through a school recognized by the Yoga Alliance.

However, these schools run a huge gamut, as the styles of yoga can vary immensely. It's also possible that there are good teachers out there who are either working towards their certification or have other credentials. For example, if they have attended some yoga teacher training workshops, have been practicing yoga for years, and hold a degree and a license in physical therapy, they probably know enough about the body to keep you safe. If a teacher seems not to know about basic anatomy, however, you should find a different one for your pose classes.

If teachers offer you medical advice, ask them where they got their information and then verify it. Remember, most yoga teachers are not naturopaths or medical doctors. Also, you will sometimes find psychobabble, pseudo-science, and new-age buzzwords in yoga classes. Don't be afraid to ask your teachers what they meant. Some teachers may repeat something they heard or read without thinking it through, but many teachers are very poetic and offer genuine words of inspiration. You will be able to tell the difference.

Even in a class focusing on poses, there is always a meditative or spiritual aspect. Some teachers are very pushy with their spiritual beliefs. Others prefer to open the door, but to let students walk through on their own—which is precisely how Punk Rock Yoga teachers teach.

# Just breathe (*pranayama*)

*Pranayama* means control of the life force, which we access most easily through control of the breath. Breath awareness and control are an integral part of the yoga pose practice. By aligning our movement with the breath in yoga poses, we focus more intently on the physical sensations of the pose. I see a remarkably practical application in breathing exercises and advocate that even if you never attempt a yoga pose, you should practice deep breathing.

When stressed, our bodies produce a fight-or-flight hormone called cortisol, which converts protein into energy. This necessary biological response helped our ancestors escape imminent danger. But too many people live in a constant state of stress with elevated cortisol levels leading to numerous health problems such as impaired thinking, poor immunity, and decreased bone mass. Deep breathing can induce the relaxation response within seconds, causing cortisol levels to drop rapidly. It's a powerful and accessible tool, but oddly an easily forgettable one. I have to remind myself to take a deep breath when dealing with my child's tantrums, but sometimes I forget and have to step out of the room first. Taking a deep breath has helped me so often in the first two years of my son's life that he imitates me by taking deep audible breaths himself.

A great exercise is to take inventory of your week and note the most stressful daily events such as commuting, dealing with certain people, etc. Then try to incorporate a few deep breaths into those moments of your day and notice how that changes your experience.

Deep breathing crosses many teachings. The self-defense courses I took at Home Alive in Seattle taught me to first stop and breathe, so I could get my head together when faced with a potential threat. Parenting books advise to take a deep breath and count to ten when parents get angry with their children. When teaching scuba diving classes, my husband instructs his students to stop everything and take at least one full breath before doing anything else in a crisis. The benefits of deep breathing have a vast reach indeed.

Aside from just deep rhythmic breathing, yoga offers numerous breathing exercises such as breathing through one nostril at a time, breathing rapidly, and making a humming sound while breathing. All have benefits and most yoga pose classes incorporate some breathing exercises into each session. Some breathing exercises—such as breath retention—work well for certain people, but are a bad idea for others, such as people with high blood pressure or women who are pregnant. Steady, rhythmic breathing is generally the best of all breathing exercises. It's called victorious breath (*ujayi pranayama*) and is the breath we use while practicing poses. Almost all meditative practices around the world utilize a form of rhythmic breathing.

If nothing else, we should practice deep breathing during stressful times. As one of my first yoga teachers often said, "The point of yoga is not to be blissed out when you're in a pretty studio surrounded by candles. The point is to keep your cool when the shit hits the fan." I could not agree more. Someday you may transcend the need to take a deep breath when stressed because you maintain equilibrium throughout every moment of your life. Most humans, however, need tools and taking a few deep breaths when angry is the most powerful hammer in our toolbox.

Though breathing is as simple as, well, breathing, many of us have no awareness of our breath. The simplest of exercises is to count your breath—inhale 1-2-3-4 and exhale 4-3-2-1. If you've never tried it, you may notice that your breath is shallow and restricted to a small part of your lungs. Deep breathing means bellowing out your entire rib cage across all three dimensions—up and down, front and back, and side to side. Imagine a balloon inflating just behind your sternum and you will get the idea. But, when you are fuming, don't worry about counting or anything like that. Just start with a few deep breaths, which will probably be rapid. Then once you feel some oxygen rushing to your brain and a bit of rational thought taking hold, practice your deep abdominal breathing with the counting.

For relaxation and clarity, I also highly recommend alternate nostril breath for everyone. Though slightly more complex, you can do it at just about any time. It takes four steps: 1) using your right thumb close your right nostril and inhale through your left nostril; 2) open your right nostril and close your left nostril with your right ring finger; then exhale through your right nostril; 3) keeping your left nostril closed, inhale through your right nostril; 4) open your left nostril and close the right, then exhale through your left nostril. An easy way to remember this breath exercise is to inhale, then switch sides. This breath is considered one of the great balancing breaths in yoga, balancing the left and right sides of our body. We will discuss the significance of the left and right sides of the body in the chapter, "Tap into your energy centers (*chakras*) and energy channels (*nadis*)." On a practical note, I practice this breath in a hot shower or sauna whenever I get a cold and find this breath truly helps clear my sinuses.

You can attach great metaphysical aspects to the breathing exercises, or you can just view them as physically beneficial. Either way, simple breathing exercises are probably the most useful, yet often-overlooked practices of yoga. Even if you never step foot in a yoga class, you should incorporate some simple breathing exercises into your daily life. If you remember nothing else about breathing, remember the axiom: "Stop, breathe, think, act."

# Go within (*pratyahara*), focus (*dharana*), and meditate (*dhyana*)

I have grouped these three limbs together because I consider them intimately related. Meditation techniques abound in numerous cultures. In yoga, the concept of meditation can vary, but many consider it a state when our mind becomes calm and still. Some consider it a cessation of thoughts, while others consider it merely a peacefulness of thoughts, letting them pass slowly by.

Buddhists often refer to a monkey mind, one that ricochets wildly from one thought to the next without any continuity, let alone resolution. In *The Yoga Sutras of Patanjali*, Patanjali describes the concept of *citta*, or disturbances in the brain. In fact, he defines yoga as "the restraint of mental fluctuations."

Two of Patanjali's eight limbs of yoga are linked tightly with meditation: withdrawal from senses (*pratyahara*) and concentration (*dharana*). These two concepts can guide you into a meditative state. Withdrawing from the senses means tuning out the sounds of traffic, the smell of a nearby bakery, and the texture of your clothing. We can easily close our eyes but not so easily shut down the four other senses, which partially explains why aspiring yogis in ancient India lived solitary existences in remote, unadorned dwellings. A yoga pose practice should heighten our senses, becoming acutely aware of our breathing and our muscle stimulation, but at the end of each session we spend our time in a final rest for time to withdraw and focus inward.

Withdrawing from the senses completely might seem dangerous—what if your smoke alarm sounded and you failed to response? My response is I doubt it. Perhaps a devout meditation practitioner might truly not hear a smoke alarm, but for most of us our reptilian brain—the brain stem responsible for self-preservation—would prevail.

Withdrawing from the senses is a valuable practice. The amount of information people process daily continues to increase exponentially, particularly for young people riveted to their cell phones following their friends' endless message flashes. This is all the more reason why at least weekly, but preferably daily, we should shut down our channels of bombardment and go within.

The next limb, concentration, is something you will easily recognize. Usually concentration involves staring at an object. For example, Tibetan Buddhist monks create elaborate paintings known as mandalas specifically for meditation. In yoga pose classes, teachers instruct students to incorporate a *drishti*, or a gaze at a particular object, to help them concentrate. However, audio input works just as well for concentration. Repetitive drumming can provide an excellent object for concentration.

Many people chant sounds or words, called *mantras*, repeatedly to induce a meditative state. These chants can also enhance concentration. Chanting the sound of AUM or OM, which represents the fundamental sound of everything around us, is often used. You can break down the chant of AUM into four parts: 1) the mouth opens wide for the "ah" sound, 2) the lips round for the "oh" sound, 3) the lips draw together for the "mmm" sound, 4) then we listen for the sound that follows—often thought of as the echo of our AUM.

Concentration and withdrawal from the senses can happen simultaneously. For example, in staring at a candle you can focus so intently that you fail to notice your neighbor's stereo playing in the distance. In fact, concentration aids withdrawing from the senses in my experience. By focusing our attention as completely as we can on one object, we can tune out distractions both external and internal. When a certain thought drags our brain in one direction, we can easily return to concentrating. Note that you do not need to concentrate on something external either—many people meditate by focusing on an image in their mind.

In the yogic definition, meditation happens after we concentrate and withdraw from the senses and empty our mind of thoughts. I see it as happening more concurrently, in that during the process of concentrating on an object and ignoring our sensory overload we are meditating.

I once asked one of my early yoga teachers how to become better at my meditative practice in final rest, or corpse pose (*savasana*). I told her I could only clear my mind of thought for maybe all of 30 seconds. She replied that if I could clear my mind of all thoughts for 30 seconds that I was doing wonderfully.

For years, I had thought the goal of yogic meditation was to clear your mind. However, one day a guest yoga teacher in my Seattle Punk Rock Yoga class disagreed with me, telling the students,

"Kimberlee says the goal is to clear your mind, but I see it as expanding your mind, and letting in all the possibilities." I will never forget that for two reasons: 1) I was thrilled that she felt comfortable enough with my class and with her convictions to disagree with me, and 2) this statement really changed how I viewed my own meditation practice.

You can think of meditation as simply emptying your mind, but there is a more realistic way of defining meditation as not dwelling on any one thought, particularly negative ones. I am certainly guilty myself of stewing about things for far too long. One of the goals of my meditation is to burn through these thoughts and try to push the anger of the past into the past. Visualizations like an ocean wave sweeping away dark thoughts can help. I also like the technique of releasing a thought with the next exhale; if a thought enters your mind you can imagine yourself blowing that thought away.

When beginning a meditation practice you should focus on releasing negative thoughts, but even positive thoughts can cloud the mind. For example, closing your eyes and giggling while remembering an amusing sitcom you watched recently is not meditation. There's nothing wrong with remembering these things, but it's not bringing you towards enlightenment or any sort of insight.

Personally, I have found practicing more active and guided meditations, particularly shamanic journeying, useful. In this Native American form, a shaman, or spiritual healer, will guide participants on a journey to what is considered the spirit realm. The leader will usually burn sage or sweet grass to help induce a meditative state, and will continually drum to help the practitioners stay focused. Leaders will suggest a mechanism, such as a canoe and a river, and guide participants through a journey. Animals have an important role in Native American spiritual systems, so participants will note what animals they encounter and the leader will then explain the significance of each animal in a vision.

Other traditions include guided meditation. For example, Dr. Robert Thurman, a popular American Buddhist scholar, has led a meditation called the jewel tree at countless gatherings. In Christian meditation, practitioners concentrate on a single thought, usually a Biblical passage, to better understand their religion's teachings. Many forms of moving meditations exist. Labyrinth walking may be more a modern phenomenon but it has roots as a Christian practice in the Middle Ages. Martial arts forms such as tai chi also provide a meditation in motion. Dance has long served as a meditative form, such as the whirling dervishes of a Sufi order in Turkey who spin their way into a trance-like state. Many modern dance teachers offer meditative dance forms, such as Gabriel Roth's 5 Rhythms method. I find my swimming provides an excellent moving meditation, as I will often silently chant a single word repeatedly. In the chapter, "Tap into your energy centers (*chakras*) and energy channels (*nadis*)," I will introduce a meditation you may find useful that involves the *chakras*.

Yoga pose classes are often called a moving meditation, and I agree. At the end of yoga classes, teachers offer a final rest, a time for meditation. Many people practice a seated meditation after practicing yoga poses, but meditation can be practiced without the poses as well. In the *Hatha Yoga Pradipika*, you will find recommended poses for seated meditation; however, finding a comfortable seated position that you can hold for several minutes without fidgeting works fine. I recommend keeping your back against a wall and sitting on a pillow to elevate your hips—both assist with posture.

Breathing is integral to meditation, and not just in the yogic tradition. Maintaining a breath rhythm helps the brain move from the beta wave pattern—characterized by alertness and activity—into an alpha pattern—characterized by relaxed, creative thought. We spend the majority of our waking time in the beta state, which enables us to grocery shop and house clean, but it is also our anxiety state. Some advanced meditation practitioners claim to enter theta waves, the dream-state we pass through on the way to deep sleep, and delta waves, the state of deep sleep. Personally, I find that goal unnecessary, as we enter those states while sleeping anyway. However, most people do lack enough time in alpha state, a state of relaxation where thoughts flow in a stream of consciousness, or what psychologist and author Mihaly Csikszentmihalyi calls flow. Though he describes this concept in terms of work—enjoying a state of total concentration where time, physical discomfort, and other normal concerns fall to the wayside (in yogic terms, withdrawing from the senses)—I see a definite correlation between his definition of flow and the alpha wave state we can reach through meditation.

In fact, a study released in 2004 of Buddhist monks demonstrated that sustained long-term meditation practice can not only alter the brain wave patterns during meditation but also can affect brain wave patterns during a resting state. In the study, monks practiced a non-referential meditation characterized by not concentrating on a single object but rather on a general sense of compassion. Researchers found their gamma oscillations—a high frequency brain wave thought to provide intense focus—to be higher in the monks than in the control group both before, during, and after the participants meditated. That meditation can account for such a fundamental difference in how our brain works is astounding.

However, finding the time and commitment to meditate can be difficult. Start with a realistic goal of once a week and pick a realistic time—don't say you will meditate every Monday morning right before work if you are typically frantic at that time. Mornings are, however, preferable to evening because our brains are fresh and not rehashing thoughts of the day. Traditionally, yogis would practice their yoga poses and meditation before dawn. The best way to start is to set aside an extra five minutes after practicing yoga poses, or, if you don't want to work on any yoga poses, dedicating five minutes at the same time every day to meditation.

A very simple meditation involves closing your eyes and following your breath. You can count the pace of the breath in your head (inhale 1-2-3-4 and exhale 4-3-2-1) or just concentrate on the word "inhale" as you breathe in and "exhale" as you breathe out. The words "in" and "out" work well, too. Eventually you can drop the words or the counts and just concentrate on the sensation of the breath. When thoughts enter your mind, release them with each exhale. Try this for a few minutes every day.

# Unmask the aspects of nature (*gunas*) and face your character (*dosha*)

Yogic philosophy identifies three faces of the natural world, called *gunas*. The behavior and characteristics of everything we can see, feel, touch, taste, and smell falls into three categories: action (*rajas*), inertia (*tamas*), and purity (*sattva*). One category will be dominant, but usually some component of all three tendencies can be found in everything around us—food, activities, elements, and even our own behavior. The goal is to balance our action and inertia until we can find the middle path, the one of purity. Excess on either side causes problems—too much activity leaves us over-stimulated, whereas too much leisure leaves us lethargic. A good way to look at our lives is to see if we are on the *sattva* track with our daily activities and seek some balance. Certain foods, such as white rice, are considered *sattvic*, which is one of the reasons white rice accompanies so many Indian meals.

Yogic philosophy also provides an interesting perspective on personality archetypes and general tendencies of our body (*doshas*), which can give us insight into our own behaviors. The three *doshas*—*vata*, *pitta*, and *kapha*—are composed of five major elements in Indian philosophy: *vata* is space (or ether) and air, *pitta* is fire and water, and *kapha* is earth and water. The Indian medical philosophy of Ayurveda is based upon this principle and seeks to balance these three humors in the body.

Everyone has some combination of all three *doshas*, with one being dominant at birth—which is our natural tendency—but another one may dominate at a different point in our lives. These temperaments manifest in both body types and personality types. People with dominant *vata* tend towards thin and sometimes weak bodies. They work and move quickly, and have great imaginations. People with dominant *pitta* tend to have medium builds. They have fiery personalities characterized by extreme mood swings, but show great commitment to working. People with dominant *kapha* tend to be heavy-set with strong bodies. They are slow to change, but are reliable and compassionate. Note not one of these is desirable over another. The trouble is that we can sometimes overload our dominant characteristic, which throws our system out of balance.

In Ayurveda, food helps us balance our bodily and mental functions. I find the Ayurvedic philosophy on food one of the most practical and useful aspects of the teaching. For example, if you feel sluggish, cut back on fats and sweets, which tend to increase *kapha*; if you feel easily angered, eat cooling foods like mangoes, which can calm *pitta* temperaments; and if you feel frenetic, eat hot, thick foods such as oatmeal, which can ground *vata*.

Ayurvedic cooking involves the concept of six tastes. At every meal you should consume all of the following flavors: bitter (leafy greens), astringent (beans, artichokes), pungent (hot peppers, garlic), sweet (fruits, sugar), salty (pickles), and sour (citrus fruits). You can incorporate all six tastes by adding spices or including condiments with your meals. I have personally noticed that if I have a dinner missing one of these components then I frequently crave something with that missing taste afterwards. What I like about the six-taste approach to diet is not only its simplicity, but also its emphasis on food as healing, rather than food as "guilty pleasure."

Your physical yoga practice can serve to balance your temperament as well. A good way to think about this is do the opposite of what you are feeling. When you are feeling sluggish, an invigorating series of yoga flows provides energy. When you are feeling flighty, balance poses help ground you. When you are feeling angered, supported forward bends can calm you down. This is far more easily said than done, of course, because we tend to gravitate towards the very thing that flares up our *dosha* tendency. My strongest temperament is *pitta*, and I am drawn to saunas, hot yoga, hot peppers, etc.— everything that aggravates *pitta*. So to balance, I incorporate swimming and lots of cucumbers.

You can use the concepts of *gunas* and *doshas* to analyze life circumstances, such where you reside. As a person whose main temperament is *pitta* followed by *vata*, I tend to be very passionate and high-change. Living in Seattle for ten years, I often felt misplaced because I consider it to be a *tamasic* city, steady and slow to change, and felt much more "at home" in places like New York, which I consider *rajasic*. I sometimes viewed Seattle as dragging me down, but I now view it as tempering me, as I may have rapidly combusted in a more frenetic city.

You can use these concepts to balance your work and personal life as well. For example, if you work as a computer programmer, I consider your job a combination of *kapha* and *vata*—physically sluggish but mentally cerebral. So a warming, energizing yoga practice would round out your day. But if you work as a defense attorney, your job requires the passion of *pitta*, so a cooling practice may serve you well.

While I do not believe in rigid adherence to Ayurveda, I do find the concepts of *gunas* and *doshas* a good paradigm for understanding how our physical and mental balance can get out of whack. Someday when you are curious, take a *dosha* quiz to gain some insight into your natural tendencies. Numerous free quizzes are available on the internet, including one listed in the "Resources" section of this book.

# Tap into your energy centers (*chakras*) and energy channels (*nadis*)

The original yoga pose practice—*hatha yoga*—focused on the concept of energy. Practitioners believed in the concept of *kundalini*—that at the base of our spine sits a feminine power, which can rise up to the crown of our head and unite with a masculine power, and this unification brings us liberation. This feminine power, depicted as a serpent coiled three times, is said to rise up through seven energy clusters along the spine, called *chakras* (translated as wheels). Each energy center has an assigned color and sound, along with psychological attributes. Only when we clear enough space in these energy centers through the yoga pose work can the feminine power rise up through all seven.

While *chakras* do not physically exist—if we performed a biopsy we would not see a green ball of spinning light in our heart—they do provide an intriguing self-diagnostic tool. They allow us to examine the health of our spine in addition to the balance of important psychological characteristics. They also provide a meditation tool and can form the basis for a physical pose practice. Let's outline them:

- root (*muladhara*): located at the base of the spine, color is red, sound is "LAHM," associated with stability and security;

- sacral (*svadhisthana*): located in the pelvis, color is orange, sound is "VAHM," associated with sexuality and creativity;

- solar plexus (*manipura*): located in the center of the abdomen, color is yellow, sound is "RAHM," associated with power, strength, and commitment;

- heart (*anahata*): located in the heart, color is green, sound is "YAHM," associated with love and compassion;

- throat (*vishuddha*): located in the throat, color is blue, sound is "HAHM," associated with truth and communication;

- brow (*ajna*): located in the center of the forehead, color is purple, sound is "AUM," associated with inner wisdom and mysticism and also called the third-eye that can see beyond the physical realm;

- crown (*sahasrara*): located at the top of the head, color is white although sometimes depicted as indigo or a spectrum of color, sound can also be "AUM" but most often is silence, associated with connecting to a universal, eternal spirit.

The goal of balancing these energies is to make sure none of them are dominant or dormant. One way to use this as a meditation tool is to visualize each area as a spinning ball of light in the color associated with that area. Start by imagining a red ball of light spinning at the base of your spine, then orange at the sacral area, yellow at the solar plexus area, green at the heart, blue at the throat, and purple at the brow. Next, imagine all the spinning balls of light spinning with equal speed and luminosity. Then you can visualize a brilliant white light radiating from the top of your head—some depict it as illuminated lotus petals.

When I practice this visualization, I often find that a *chakra* center that seems dull or slow usually corresponds to a current psychological imbalance I am having in that area. You can use this meditation technique proactively as well. For example, if you find yourself struggling to communicate with others, you can focus your meditation on the throat center.

If you want to add sound to your meditative practice you can chant the sounds associated with each center. I also like to chant a word that represents the psychological aspect as well. As you chant, you can focus your thoughts on each area. Beginning with the base of your spine chant "LAHM" and "stable," then at the sacral area chant "VAHM" and "creative," at the solar plexus area "RAHM" and "strong," at the heart "YAHM" and "loving," at the throat "HAHM" and "honest," at the brow "AUM" and "wise," and at the crown stop and enjoy the silence. You can also run through all the sounds on one long exhaling breath: "LAHM-VAHM-RAHM-YAHM-HAHM-AUM."

Physically, you can work through this list by picking yoga poses that focus on each area and work your way from bottom to top. I sometimes use this framework to sequence my personal pose practice. Here is a sequence I frequently use:

- root: chair pose (*utkatasana*) and downward facing dog (*adho mukha svanasana*);

- sacral: tree (*vrksasana*) and pigeon (*kapotasana*);

- solar plexus: boat (*navasana*) and upward facing dog (*urdhva mukha svanasana*);

- heart: bridge with hands clasped underneath (*setu bandha sarvangasana*) and eagle (*garudasana*);

- throat: fish (*matsyasana*) and neck stretches;

- brow: supported shoulder stand (*salamba sarvangasana*) and child's pose (*balasana*);

- crown: head stand (*salamba sirsasana*) and seated meditation.

I suggest warming up first before this special sequence. If you have not encountered these poses, one of your yoga pose class teachers will assist you. If you have not taken any classes, not to worry—you can think about exercises or stretches for each area as well. For example, for the sacral area region you can circle the hips, and for the heart center you can circle the shoulders. Notice the areas where you struggle and think about your current life situation. If the solar plexus region challenges you, examine how often you have committed to something, how often you have stood up for yourself, etc. I'm not saying that strengthening your belly muscles will turn you into a warrior, but there is a lot to be said about postural strength—standing up straight not only projects confidence externally it also creates confidence within.

Unfortunately, the concept of *chakras* has become overly commodified: you can purchase chakra tea, chakra yoga pants, chakra candles, etc. I know you are savvy enough to know that burning a red candle will not transform your life, but I find *chakras* an interesting framework for self-examination and meditation.

Related to the *chakras* is the concept of *nadis*, or energy channels. You can consider them similar to meridians, which govern the practice of acupuncture. In yogic theory of anatomy, there are numerous minor channels and three major channels: *ida*, which runs on the left side of the body and is considered downward flowing and cooling; *pingala*, which runs on the right side of the body and is considered upward flowing and heating; and *sushumna*, which is the central channel and is considered neutral. Returning to the concept of *kundalini*, it's through the central *sushumna* channel where the feminine power rises up to unite with the masculine.

A practical application of energy channels is the concept of balance. Aggressiveness and receptiveness are not bad traits in and of themselves, but an excess of either causes harm. You can imagine that you have two currents flowing in your body at all times and you want to keep both currents flowing without overloading the circuitry. In yogic philosophy, the nostrils represent whether the currents are open or blocked. Alternate nostril breath, as discussed in the "Just breathe (*pranayama*)" chapter, addresses this very issue of opening both nostrils to balance the body. Another way to balance these channels is to incorporate cross-lateral movement—for example, reaching your right hand towards your left foot, and vice-versa. Twist poses in yoga, such as lying spinal twist (*supta matsyendrasana*), incorporate cross-lateral positions. The concept of *nadis* reminds us that the goal of yoga is balance and to find the middle path between extremes.

# Find liberation (*samadhi*)

We have circled around the concept of liberation throughout the book, so we should now discuss what it really means. This is difficult for me to verbalize because liberation is not quantifiable. To paraphrase former U.S. Supreme Court Justice Potter Stewart, I cannot intelligently define it, but I know it when I see it.

I will attempt to begin the discussion by categorizing the two ways in which I view liberation: permanent and temporary.

Classic yogic texts describe yogis who permanently liberate themselves from the bonds of past action (*karma*), from worldly concerns, and from anything that drags them down. These yogis were called *jivanmukti*, or living saints. Many yogis also believe in reincarnation and believe that the ultimate goal is to achieve a perfect state of liberation where you no longer need to be born again (*moksha*).

I view liberation in a much subtler way, and as more of a temporary state. This liberation, where we transcend every biological impulse and every mundane thought, is like a butterfly. It will land upon you for an instant, and if you are very quiet and still it may linger long enough for you to notice. I cannot describe what liberation feels like for others. I can only share my own glimpse into transcendence, which, frankly, is difficult to put into words. I perceive it as absolute serenity, quiet, peace, and joy, where my normal concerns, aches, and pains fade into obscurity.

Liberation is just one limb of the royal yoga system, and I envision all eight limbs as components that operate in a circular pattern. By practicing the restraints and actions you sweep aside impediments to personal serenity and free up time and space for your pose, breath, and meditative practices. By practicing the poses, breathwork, and meditation, you foster tranquility and liberation, which in turn helps you practice the restraints and actions.

One hope is that the more we can feel this sense of liberation during our meditative practices, the more joy we can feel in our daily lives. I see the Dalai Lama as the epitome of joy. Though not a yogi, he of course practices meditation as a Buddhist monk. Ever modest, he claims he has not evolved into a perfectly liberated being, but I can see that he has experienced great liberation because he radiates joy.

This should be our goal with our entire yogic practice: cultivate inner peace, which can spread into everything we do. I notice a strong difference when I let my practice slide, and I am certain you will notice a strong difference when you commit to any form of a meditative practice—focused yoga poses, rhythmic breathing, seated meditation, guided meditation, etc. If nothing else, this is a mandate to take a few minutes every day to tune out of everything that bombards us and tune into our inner sanctuary.

# Continue evolving

In this book, we have discussed the eight limbs in Patanjali's royal yoga system: restraints, actions, poses, breath and life force, withdrawal from the senses, concentration, meditation, and liberation. Also, we surveyed additional yoga concepts such as personality archetypes and energy centers.

The journey continues. I encourage you to read some classic yoga texts as listed in the "Resources" section of this book. If you currently attend yoga classes, ask your instructor philosophical questions to get his or her perspective. If you have yet to take a yoga pose class—go ahead and try it. Commit yourself to some meditation time at least once a week, if not daily.

Before you descend from the mount, I will summarize some of the wisdom I hope you have gleaned from this interpretation of yoga philosophy.

- Follow the middle path, avoiding extremes on either end.

- Be kind to yourself and to others.

- Live in the moment, letting the past stay in the past while knowing you will meet the future sooner than you realize.

- Enjoy all that you have and all that you are, accepting that you can find happiness even without everything that you see, hear, smell, taste, and touch.

- Keep your body active to keep your mind sharp.

- Think deeply, and often, but do not dwell once you have reached resolution.

- Seek a greater truth beyond your day-to-day concerns

- And finally, if I could summarize it in one catch phrase: "Look, work, accept, transcend."

# Appendix: a brief history of yoga

Yoga has flourished for more than 5,000 years. The Western world's first major encounter happened in 1893 when Swami Vivekananda presented a yoga discourse at the World Parliament of Religions in Chicago. It crept its way into Western pop culture in the 1960s when musicians and celebrities embraced meditation, then exploded in the 1990s when yoga pose classes appeared on fitness club schedules across the United States. But we need to back up several millennia to understand the context of yoga.

Yoga is one of several schools of ancient Indian philosophy, all of which were an attempt to understand the nature of reality and existence. Here is a summary of the six major schools of Indian philosophy:

- The Nyaya philosophy proclaims that knowledge is obtained through four sources—perception, inference, comparison, and oral testimony—and that logical thinking leads to the cessation of suffering.

- The Vaisheshika school of thought believes that all objects in the known universe can be reduced down to a finite number of atoms, which are controlled by an all-powerful being.

- Samkhya is a dualistic school of thought which sees the world in two planes: *prakriti*, the physical world; and *purusha*, a higher consciousness. This concept of a person's spirit as separate from the corporal body carries over to the world of yoga.

- Raja Yoga (or royal yoga) is a mental discipline aimed towards achieving liberation. This tradition incorporates the theories of Samkhya.

- Purva Mimamsa involves ritualistic following of the Vedas— literature written in Sanskrit and the basis for Hinduism.

- Vedanta (also known as Uttara Mimamsa) is another school based on the Vedas with the inclusion of the Upanishads—a body of literature that spans centuries. Followers of Vedanta aim to realize their true human nature, which is considered divine.

Raja Yoga evolved along with these five other schools of thought, and is tightly bound with Samkhya. Archeological finds indicate the people in the Indus Valley were practicing yoga poses as early as the period of 3300–1700 BC.

The definitive yoga texts were written in the Sanskrit language, an ancient Indian language and a basis for modern day Hindi, similar to how Latin begat Italian. The word "yoga" translates to "to yoke" or "to unite." Through yoga, a practitioner attempts to unite the self with the sacred. However, what is sacred is not strictly defined. In fact, even in the Hindu religion the pantheon of gods are not seen as the ultimate divinity, but rather as manifestations of aspects of a greater power.

This, of course, raises the question: does practicing yoga mean practicing Hinduism? While the origins of yoga and Hinduism bear many similarities, and many Hindus practice yoga, and some yoga poses are named for Hindu figures, yoga itself does not impose a specific belief system. Yogic philosophy does attempt to answer the question, "What is the meaning of life?" and define the nature of reality—which we discuss in the chapter, "Get real"—but it does not prescribe the worship of any deity.

Instead of binding yoga to Hinduism or regarding it as a religion, a more accurate way to think about yogic philosophy is to compare it to Western schools of philosophy. I often compare it to transcendentalism, a movement in the 19th century United States which proposed that a universal spirit transcends all organized religion and that only through introspection can one realize this spiritual truth. Ralph Waldo Emerson and Henry David Thoreau both subscribed to this philosophy and advocated reflecting in natural settings, not unlike the prescriptions for meditation given by yoga instructors. As Emerson wrote in his essay *Nature*, "The happiest man is he who learns from nature the lesson of worship."

The first place to look at how yogic philosophy attempts to explain our existence is the *Yoga Sutras of Patanjali*. This book is a compilation of passages compiled by an ancient yogi named Patanjali in what scholars date as the second century B.C. The term *sutra* means "thread" in Sanskrit. The original writing is terse by design because the tradition was that the guru gave the aspiring yogi concise threads of wisdom, and the yogi's job was to spend hours weaving the threads together through contemplation.

In the book, Patanjali outlines an eight-step plan for liberation, referred to as the eight limbs of yoga, or *astanga* yoga. (Note there is a vigorous pose practice also called astanga, which involves lots of flowing from pose to pose with the breath. One does not need to perform the pose practice called astanga to be practicing the eight-limbed path of Patanjali.) These eight limbs are summarized in the chapter, "Discover the eight limbs."

Though a great deal of the *Yoga Sutras of Patanjali* contains esoteric philosophy, which can be difficult to truly absorb, the eight limbs provide not only guidelines for a meditative practice, but also considerations for leading a peaceful, and hopefully better life. Much of the *Punk Rock Yoga Manifesto* is based upon my interpretations of the eight limbs, cultivated through study and my own reflection. Because the *sutras* are so terse, the interpretations can vary widely. While this often makes for controversy, it also keeps yogic philosophy alive and engaging.

Some yogis believed the path Patanjali outlined is rigid in the sense that the eight steps had to be practiced in order. Personally, I do not read that in the text, but respect that the ancient oral traditions may have enforced that. However, many yogis decided to turn the Patanjali tradition on its head. Instead of believing that you should master the psychological aspects of yoga before beginning the pose and meditative practices, they believed that by performing meditative poses, breathing exercises, and cleansing practices, a person will naturally begin the psychological evolution prescribed by the first two limbs. I find some logic to this line of thinking—if a person feels his needs are being met, including taking time for himself physically and spiritually, most likely that person will begin to treat others with greater compassion and decency.

These yogis decided that the psychological discipline in Patanjali's system presented an unnecessary barrier to practicing yoga so they created their own system called hatha yoga. This was first captured in *Hatha Yoga Pradipika,* written by Swami Swatmarama in the 15th century. Forming the basis for almost every yoga class out there, this book presents three fundamental aspects of yoga: physical postures, breathing exercises, and cleansing routines.

The guiding principle behind hatha yoga is the balance or unification of sun (*ha*) and moon (*tha*) energies. While these energies are often referred to as masculine and feminine, I prefer to view them not as male and female but rather as aggressive and receptive qualities. Both traits are beneficial and necessary when they balance each other, which is precisely what hatha yoga strives to accomplish. This is similar to the tantric philosophy, which influenced the hatha yoga movement.

Tantra practitioners believe there are two divine powers—Shiva, the masculine sitting at the crown of the head, and Shakti, the feminine sitting at the base of the spine—and the goal is to unite these energies. The practice of kundalini yoga is focused on achieving liberation by uniting these two energies.

*Hatha Yoga Pradipika* operates from the premise that if you first care for your body and your mind, naturally your behavior will evolve. However, I believe that both the physical and behavioral improvements can and should be done concurrently.

Additional bodies of literature have also influenced modern yoga. Many people will reference the *Bhagavad Gita*—a parable of a discussion between the Hindu deity Krishna and a warrior named Arjuna during an epic battle, which symbolizes the battle for control of Arjuna's spirit. Krishna relays to Arjuna numerous paths of yoga, such as service, devotion, and knowledge. While this text certainly influenced the work of Patanjali, for me it crosses the line between yoga as a secular spiritual practice and yoga as a Hindu ritual; I'm sure many yogis may disagree. The *Bhagavad Gita* is certainly worth reading, but I consider the *Yoga Sutras of Patanjali* and the *Hatha Yoga Pradipika* much more descriptive of a mental and physical discipline, rather than a practice linked with religion.

Hatha yoga regained popularity in the 1930s through the teachings of Sri T. Krishnamacharya, who lectured throughout India. Major influences on modern yoga have come from him and four of his students—Indra Devi, Sri K. Pattabhi Jois, B.K.S. Iyengar, and T.K.V. Desikachar.

Indra Devi was instrumental in opening yoga to women and in 1947 founded a popular yoga studio in Hollywood. She spread her teachings of yoga throughout Europe and North and South America for many decades, beginning in the 1950s.

In 1948, Sri K. Pattabhi Jois founded an institute in India for the astanga yoga style, which is characterized by well-defined flowing sequences. Numerous current teachers have adopted this style, and it has spawned a movement characterized by more diversity of sequences called vinyasa yoga.

B.K.S. Iyengar, for whom Iyengar yoga is named, brought his yoga teaching to Europe in the 1950s. In 1966 he wrote *Light on Yoga*, which many teachers call the "yoga bible" because of the extensive pose descriptions and photographs. While I appreciate that work as a reference, it contains numerous poses that require extreme flexibility, which can be daunting for a beginner. In 2005 Iyengar wrote *Light on Life* and while promoting it he joked that no one should listen to what he had to say in *Light on Yoga* because at the time he was a young man who knew nothing.

T.K.V. Desikachar, the son and student of Krishnamacharya, founded the Krishnamacharya Yoga Mandiram organization in 1976. This organization implemented a style called Viniyoga that incorporates adaptations of poses based on physical ability and has greatly influenced other styles in this regard. He later dropped the name Viniyoga and instead uses the name of Krishnamacharya for his teachings. Viniyoga was subsequently trademarked by his student, Gary Kraftsow, who continues the traditions of the style.

Many other yoga teachers in India have also had a great influence on contemporary yoga. The book *Autobiography of a Yogi* written by Paramahansa Yogananda in 1946 introduced people around the world to a meditation technique called kriya yoga, which involves extensive breath control exercises.

Sri Swami Satchidananda was another influential teacher who in 1966 founded the Integral Yoga organization in New York City. In addition to providing well-known translations and commentaries of the *Yoga Sutras of Patanjali* and the *Bhagavad Gita*, he has authored several other books. To those outside the yoga community, he was best known for being the opening speaker at the first Woodstock music festival.

On an interesting and I believe non-coincidental note, Krishnamacharya passed away at the age of 100, Devi at 102, Jois at 93, and Satchidananda at 88; and at this writing, Desikachar and Iyengar are alive and practicing yoga at ages 73 and 91, respectively.

# Resources

The following resources may help you develop your own practice. There are numerous resources on yoga out there, but here's a quick list to get you started.

## Books

*Dharma Punx* by Noah Levine

*Hatha Yoga Pradipika* by Swami Muktibodhananda

*Maps to Ecstasy: The Healing Power of Movement* by Gabrielle Roth

*Yoga Anatomy* by Leslie Kaminoff

The *Yoga Sutras of Patanjali* translation and commentary by Sri Swami Satchidananda

## DVDs

*A.M. and P.M. Yoga for Beginners* by Rodney Yee, Patricia Walden, and Steve Adams

*Forrest Yoga 5-Day Audio CD Intensive Course* by Ana Forrest

*River Flow: Level I* by Tias Little

*Vinyasa Flow Session I DVD: Uniting Movement and Breath* by Seane Corn

## Web sites

| | |
|---|---|
| Punk Rock Yoga: | PunkRockYoga.com |
| 8th Element Yoga: | 8thElementYoga.com |
| Dosha quiz: | DoshaQuiz.Chopra.com |
| Street Yoga: | StreetYoga.org |
| Yoga basics: | YogaBasics.com |
| Yoga history: | PurePrana.com/yoga/styles.html |
| *Yoga Journal*: | YogaJournal.com |
| Yoga videos: | YogaVibes.com |

# About the author

Kimberlee Jensen Stedl founded Punk Rock Yoga® in 2003. Kimberlee first took up yoga in 1997 at the behest of a yoga teacher whose class followed the kickboxing class Kimberlee taught at a Seattle gym. She was instantly humbled and intrigued. Over the years, Kimberlee has tasted numerous flavors of yoga including Iyengar, vinyasa, Viniyoga, Bikram, and kundalini yoga. When she decided to pursue teaching, she achieved her Yoga Alliance 200-hour Registered Yoga Teacher credentials through the YogaFit program. During her teacher training she began her study of yoga philosophy. As she continues to work on those principles she realizes she should wear a t-shirt saying, "Caution: evolving soul under construction. Beware of flying debris."

Before Kimberlee was introduced to yoga, she worked as a fitness instructor. She earned her group fitness instructor certification with the American Council on Exercise (ACE) in 1992 and with the Aerobics and Fitness Association of America (AFAA) in 2007. She has also offered fitness instructor continuing education courses accredited by both ACE and AFAA. She offers teacher training in her signature yoga and dance fusion style called Shake Rattle & Pose®. Kimberlee established 8th Element Yoga (www.8thElementYoga.com) in 2007 to support her diverse yoga interests.

Kimberlee has a bachelor's degree in Journalism, which has served her writing endeavors. She has co-authored two yoga books with her husband Todd: *Yoga for Scuba Divers* and their partner yoga book, *Yoga with a Friend*. Together, Kimberlee and Todd offer yoga and scuba diving retreats. Of course, their biggest co-creation is their son Ivan, born in 2008—an event which taught Kimberlee the true meaning of radical transformation.

You can reach Kimberlee at yoga@PunkRockYoga.com

Made in the USA
Coppell, TX
03 March 2022

74432129R00056